A Life of Our Lord
for Children

MARIGOLD HUNT

A Life of Our Lord
for Children

SOPHIA INSTITUTE PRESS®
Manchester, New Hampshire

Sophia Institute Press®
Box 5284, Manchester, NH 03108
1-800-888-9344
www.sophiainstitute.com

Nihil obstat:
Arthur J. Scanlan, S.T.D.
Censor Librorum

Imprimatur:
Francis J. Spellman
Archbishop, New York
New York, June 16, 1939

Library of Congress Cataloging-in-Publication Data

Hunt, Marigold.
   A life of our Lord for children / Marigold Hunt.
      p. cm.
   Originally published: New York : Sheed & Ward, 1939.
   Summary: Describes the life of Jesus Christ and the establishment of his Kingdom as the Catholic Church.
   ISBN 1-928832-64-4 (alk. paper)
   1. Jesus Christ—Biography—Juvenile literature. [1. Jesus Christ. 2. Catholic Church. 3. Christianity.] I. Title.
BT302.H87 2003
232.9'01—dc22   2003018721

28th printing

Contents

A Life of Our Lord
for Children

One

The Church Is the Kingdom

What is the Church we belong to? Is it just like other people's churches, only the right one? No, it is much more than that. It is a kingdom, the kingdom of Christ the King.

This book is about how the King came into this world and about the Kingdom He founded while He was here. It does not tell you all about the things He did. There is only room in a small book for a few of them; but when you have read it you will know at least one very important thing about Him — and about us. He did found a Kingdom, and it is to that Kingdom that all of us belong.

Some countries have kings ruling over them, some have presidents, some have still other arrangements. But in whatever way the country we belong to is managed, we all belong to the Kingdom our Lord founded; it is called the Catholic Church.

Two

Before the King Came

You know that God made the world we live in, and the sun and stars and everything else that we can see, besides all the other things that we cannot see. He made them perfectly, and He was pleased with what He had done. Then He made Adam and Eve, a man and a woman, and put them to rule over His world and to look after it and enjoy it.

But Adam and Eve fell into sin — the first and worst of all the sins in the world; it spoiled everything, and made the whole world begin to go wrong. If only they had behaved themselves, we would have had no pain or sorrow or worry, and we would have gone straight to Heaven when we died. It is a pity they sinned, isn't it?

But they were sorry, and as soon as they had told God so, He promised that it would all come right some-day because He would send Somebody who would make up for what they had done. But they did not know when this would happen or that the Person who came to save the world would be God Himself.

Now, if God was to come into the world, the world had to be made ready to receive Him. If men were not to forget all about Him, and about the promise of a Savior in the meantime, there had to be some people in the world whose special business it was to remember those things.

God arranged for this by choosing a family who were the beginning of a whole race of people, the same people we call Jews. The race that this family grew into called themselves the Chosen People, because God had chosen them to keep alive the two great truths: that there is one God — not no god or dozens of gods, as people always begin to think if they are left to themselves — and that there was Somebody coming who would be of their race and who would save the world.

The first part of the Bible is called the Old Testament, and it is all about the things that happened to the Chosen People and how God dealt with them. In it you can read about all kinds of curious men and women who led very adventurous and interesting lives.

I have to tell you a little about them here; otherwise reading our Lord's life will be like coming into a movie when it is half-finished, and never finding out what happened in the first part.

Abraham is the first of them. God told him that his descendants would possess a beautiful new country and that they would grow to be so many that they would be as uncountable as the stars in the sky. Abraham had a son called Isaac, to whom God repeated these promises, and Isaac had a son called Jacob, who was given them again, too. These three, Abraham, Isaac, and Jacob, are the ancestors of all the Chosen People.

There is something else you should know about Jacob. His name was changed to Israel, and that is how the Chosen People came later on to be called Israelites, or just Israel. Jacob, who was called Israel, had twelve sons, and one of them was called Joseph. Jacob's other sons were very jealous of Joseph; in fact they couldn't stand him, so they sold him as a slave to traders who were going into Egypt, and told his father that he had been killed.

Joseph did so well there that he became the greatest man in Egypt except for Pharaoh. (The kings of the Egyptians were called pharaohs.) So when presently there was a famine in the country where his father and brothers lived, they were thankful to be allowed to come and live in Egypt, too.

When Jacob was dying he foretold what would happen to the descendants of each of his twelve sons. One of his sons was called Judah; the prophecy for him was that when the Chosen People had kings, they would all be descended from Judah, right down to the time when the promised Savior came.

Well, Jacob's descendants stayed in Egypt for a long time. Presently there came to be such a lot of them that the Egyptians began to think that soon there would be no room in the country for anyone else. Then a pharaoh who knew nothing about Joseph came to the throne; he was very hard and unjust to the Chosen People, and passed a terrible law that all their boy babies were to be killed as soon as they were born. But it is easier to make a law like that than to get people to keep it, and a lot of boy babies were allowed to live.

One of the babies who lived to grow up was given the name Moses. When Moses was a baby, his mother put him in a basket and hid him in the bulrushes along the edge of a river where Pharaoh's own daughter found him. She took Moses home and raised him herself.

When Moses had grown up, God chose him to lead His Chosen People out of Egypt and into the land He had promised to Abraham so long ago. When it was time to begin doing this, God spoke to Moses and told him His plan. Moses was an astonishing person. He was afraid to do what God asked him, but he was not afraid to ask God  what His name was. God gave him this mysterious and interesting answer, "*I am who am*," and He said that the Israelites were always to remember that that was what God should be called.

Then Moses said, "I can't go and make Pharaoh let Your people go, because I stammer, and can't talk impressively!" So God let him take his brother Aaron with him to do the talking.

I wish that I could tell you the whole story of all the things that Moses and Aaron said to Pharaoh, and of all the terrible things God made happen to the Egyptians before they would let the Israelites go. You see, the Egyptians found the Israelites very useful as slaves, and although they did not want too many of them, they did not at all want to lose them altogether. So God made nine Terrible Things, which are called the Plagues of

Egypt, happen one after the other. When Pharaoh still wouldn't let the Israelites go, God told Moses to warn him that He was going to send an angel at midnight to kill the eldest sons of all the Egyptian women. But Pharaoh wouldn't listen.

Then Moses went to the Chosen People and told them what was to happen and what God had arranged for them to do on the night when the Egyptians' sons were killed.

Each family was to take a lamb and kill it in the evening, and they were to mark the posts of their doors with its blood.

That night they were to eat the lamb, roasted, with unleavened bread and wild lettuce. And they were to eat standing up, already dressed for a journey, because they must leave the instant Pharaoh sent word that they might go.

Roast meat cooks faster than boiled; wild lettuce needn't be cooked at all; and unleavened bread, which means bread made without any yeast to raise it, is much quicker to make than the ordinary sort. Everything had to be done in a hurry.

That night the angel came and killed the eldest sons of all the Egyptians. But where he saw lamb's blood marking the door of a house, he knew that it belonged to the Chosen People, and passed over it without hurting anyone inside.

God told Moses that the Chosen People were to keep a feast every year in memory of that night when He brought them out of the land of Egypt, and when the angel of death "passed over" their houses. And so they did, and the Jews all over the world still do, and they call this feast the Passover, because of the angel that "passed over" their houses.

When the Egyptians discovered in the night that all their eldest sons were dead, even Pharaoh's heir, they implored the Chosen People to go out of Egypt at once, and take everything they possessed. So all the Chosen People set out on the instant and left Egypt after they had been there 430 years, Moses and Aaron leading them out into the desert on their way to the Promised Land at last.

I wish, too, that I could tell you all that happened to them in the desert. They were there for forty years, not because it is a very large desert, but because there was a great deal that God wanted them to learn on their way and also because they behaved very badly. You see, God had provided them with a special kind of food, something like bread, called "manna," and instead of being grateful, they said they wanted meat, too! And they were always asking to go back to Egypt again, and reminding each other of all the good things they had had to eat while they were there, and quite forgetting what is was like to be slaves.

In the desert there is a mountain called Mount Sinai, and Moses went up onto it alone, and there God gave him the Ten Commandments. One of them, as I am sure you know, is the commandment to keep holy the Sabbath Day, which is Saturday, the seventh day of the week. God said it must be that day, because when He made the world, He made it in six days and rested on the seventh. (Nobody knows how long those six days were, in which God made the world; but that doesn't matter, we know how long our kind of days are.)

Moses went up into the mountain again, and God told him how He was to be worshiped, and that He wanted a Tabernacle made for Him. *Tabernacle* means tent, and, while the Israelites were traveling about in a desert, it was the only kind of church they could have, wasn't it?

If you find the part of the Bible called Exodus (near the beginning) and look at Chapter 25 you will find the directions God gave Moses for making the Tabernacle.

They are very particular directions. God told Moses exactly which parts of it were to be made of wood and which of silver and precious stones, and how big and what shape it was to be. He told him also how the vestments used in worshiping Him were to be made, for the Chosen People's priests had to have special clothes for serving Him, just as our priests have special vestments for saying Mass.

The priests were to be Aaron and his sons, who were descended from Levi, one of Jacob's sons. They were to offer sacrifices to God and look after the Tabernacle. A lamb was to be offered every morning and every evening, and incense every morning and every evening, too. It seems to us very odd, now, that God would have wanted a lamb, or any kind of animal, killed in His honor; that is because we are used to the idea of our Lord's sacrifice, which was so great and perfect that it did away with the need for all such offerings.

The idea of wanting to offer things to God and of destroying in His honor what we would like to have had for ourselves, goes back to the beginning of the world. Adam's sons, Cain and Abel, offered sacrifice. The idea of sacrifice not only goes back to the very beginning, but it is all over the world, too. As soon as people know, or guess, that there is a God who made them and everything else, they want to offer Him something, to show that they know it all belongs to Him really. The reason all men have that feeling is just that it is right. Sacrifices had always been offered, but now God regulated how it was to be done.

Moses lived to see the Promised Land, but it was another leader, Josue, who led the Chosen People into it. We call the Promised Land Palestine, and you can find it on a map of the world, in between Syria, South Arabia, and the Red Sea, which is at the very end of the Mediterranean. The Chosen People had to fight hard to take possession of it, and all this part of the Bible is full of fighting. When, with the help of God, they had won, they divided the country among them, according to which of Jacob's sons they were descended from.

The Israelites still had no kings, but now they began to have "judges" who told them when they had done wrong and how to do right, if they would, and who led them in battle, for there were still plenty of battles to be fought.

The last great judge was called Samuel. When he was old he appointed his sons as judges, but they were very bad ones, and all the people began to say, "Why can't we be like other nations and have a king?" Samuel warned them that they wouldn't like it if they had one, but God told him to make them a king anyway, as they wanted one, and He sent the man He had chosen to Samuel.

That was Saul, the first King of Israel. He was very good at winning battles, but he began to disobey God, and God told Samuel to choose someone else to be king after him. God sent Samuel to a shepherd boy called David and told him that this was the man to choose.

Of David you can read in the First Book of Kings, which you can find in the Bible. David is the person I like best in the whole Old Testament; he had the most extraordinary and exciting adventures, and although he also did some horrible things, he was always truly sorry afterward.

God Himself called David "a man after my own heart," so it can't be wrong for me to like him as well, can it?

David wrote the Psalms, which Jews and Christians both have sung ever since. After David, his son Solomon reigned, and Solomon was the wisest, richest and most magnificent king that the Israelites ever had. Although David had made ready all of the things needed for building a Temple for God, it was Solomon who had it built, in Jerusalem. The Tabernacle had been all very well in the desert, but now that they were settled down in the Promised Land, it was time to build a proper place to worship God. If you want to know how the Temple was built you can read about it in the Third Book of Kings, beginning at the fifth chapter.

It was a pity Solomon couldn't stay good after he started so well, but he didn't. He married an astonishing number of wives (people then were allowed to) and some were not Israelites, but foreigners who worshiped idols, and at last Solomon fell into that sin, too. Nobody knows whether he was sorry or not before he died.

After Solomon's death, his son Roboam was king, but a man called Jeroboam rebelled against Roboam and made himself king over all the northern part of the kingdom. So Roboam ruled only over Jerusalem and the southern part of Palestine, and the two parts never were joined again.

Presently the Assyrians, who were a mighty people with a strong army, made war against Jeroboam and defeated him. Then they carried away most of the Israelites to be slaves, and put people from other countries to live in that region and farm the land. This part of Palestine was called Samaria in our Lord's time.

In the meantime, the Southern Kingdom was having one war after another and being defeated over and over again. At last the King of Babylon came and carried the people off into captivity and destroyed Jerusalem.

He held the Chosen People captive for seventy years, and after that they were allowed to go home. As soon as they got there they began to try to rebuild the

Temple. It was at this time that they began to be called Jews, as we call them today.

The people living in what had been the Northern Kingdom were a mixture. Most of them were foreigners brought to the country by the Assyrians, but some were Israelites who had been left behind when the Assyrians took the rest of them away as captives. They thought that as they were partly Chosen People, although mixed in race and religion, they ought to be allowed to come and help to rebuild the Temple. But the Chosen People who had returned to Jerusalem were furious, and said that the people of Samaria had no right to come near the Temple, let alone to help rebuild it. This made the people of Samaria very angry, and they never forgave the insult.

The next thing that happened to poor Palestine was that Alexander the Great, the famous general from Greece, marched through it, and after that the Greeks began to take far more interest in it than the Israelites liked. At last the people of Palestine made a league with the Romans, and after more wars and troubles there was a civil war, and one side appealed to the Romans to come and help. A Roman general called Pompey captured Jerusalem sixty-four years before our Lord was born. After that the Chosen People were under Roman rule.

The Romans, you know, were very good at ruling other people's countries, and they had a very big empire. They used to let the people they governed have quite a lot of freedom to rule themselves in some ways, so that they would be content and not rebel. They could have their own law courts and decide all small matters of government. The Jewish court that did this was called the Sanhedrin. Only they couldn't put anyone to death unless the Romans had judged him too, and found him guilty. And they were allowed to run the Temple as they always had — the priests who served it still keeping the same rules as were given to Moses in the desert.

They even had a king of a sort. All through the captivity and everything else that had happened to them, they had kept on having a king who was descended from Judah. (Do you remember the prophecy Jacob made that there would always be a king descended from Judah until the Savior came?)

Well, a few years before our Lord was born, the Romans set up a king called Herod. And not only was he not descended from Judah, but he was not even a Jew! Then everyone in Jerusalem and the Holy Land who was learned in Holy Scripture began to wonder if the time of the Messiah had finally come. That is how things were at the time of our Lord's birth.

Now I have to tell you something else about God's special way of dealing with

His Chosen People. They were not always good at doing what He told them. In fact, the more He did for them the worse they got, so He sent special people, as He had sent Moses, to remind them of what He had already told them, to tell them again what they must do, and to say what would happen if they didn't change their ways.

Sometimes these special people told them, too, about things that were going to happen far off in the future. These messengers from God were called prophets and they all had a very hard time, for people would hardly ever listen to them, and generally ended by killing them outright.

But if you read the Gospels, you will see that the men who wrote them often point out that our Lord kept fulfilling the prophecies about the Great King. St. Matthew did this more than the others because he wrote his Gospel for the Jews, who knew all about prophecies. Through the prophets God told them more and more about the King who was to come, the same Savior who had been promised to Abraham and Isaac and Jacob, even to Adam and Eve.

The first two parts of God's promise to Abraham were fulfilled already — his descendants were a whole nation, and they possessed the land promised to them by God. Now what about the Great King? The prophets had other names for him besides "King." They called him the "Messiah," which means the same as "the Christ," "the Anointed One." Kings were anointed with holy oils when they were crowned, so that really it means the same thing.

When the prophets spoke of the Great King it sometimes sounded as if He would be great in the same way Solomon had been, only even richer and grander and more powerful. But sometimes it sounded as if all the King's greatness was going to be in His holiness and the most important thing about Him would be that He would save His people from their sins.

One of the prophets even foretold that He would be despised and rejected and poor. Nobody liked that. They wanted the King to be rich and grand. So they forgot about those prophecies and went on expecting a king like Solomon. And that is just what we would have done, isn't it?

But no one yet understood that it was really God Himself who would come, although there were all sorts of hints in what the prophets said. We can understand them easily enough, but if we had lived then, we would not have.

You see, the Israelites did not know about the Blessed Trinity. God had not told them that although there was only one God there were Three Persons in God — the Father, the Son, and the Holy Spirit. So they could not guess that God the Son would become man by the power of the Holy Spirit and have God the Father for His Father, could they?

We are very lucky to live now and know so much more about God than anybody did in those days, and luckier still to belong to the kingdom of God the Son.

Three

The King Comes

The pages before this were about the way in which the world was prepared for the coming of the Great King, from the days of Adam and Eve until it was almost time for Him to arrive. This part begins with the very last preparations for His coming.

In those days there was a Jewish priest called Zachary who had a wife called Elizabeth. They were both old enough to be grandparents, but they weren't, because they had never had any children, although both of them had wanted children very much.

One day Zachary went into the Temple in Jerusalem to offer incense to God. While he was there an angel came and stood on the right side of the altar.

No one who has not seen an angel knows what they look like, and no one who has seen one can describe them. But you have seen pictures of angels, and you can guess how much more magnificent a real angel of God would look. So Zachary was very much afraid, and the angel said, "Fear not, Zachary. I have come to tell you that you and Elizabeth are going to have a son and that you are to call him John. Everyone will rejoice when he is born, and he will be a very great man indeed."

But Zachary said, "Elizabeth and I are very old to be having babies. Are you sure about this?"

That was a silly thing to say to an angel, wasn't it? And after he had said it the angel gave him good reason to be frightened, saying, "I am Gabriel who stands before God; He sent me to tell you this good news. But since you can't believe me, I will give you a sign that this is true — from now until your son is born, you will not be able to speak." Then the angel went away, and Zachary came out of the Temple, and, sure enough, he couldn't speak a word, and so he had to write or make signs whenever he wanted to say anything.

Zachary's wife, Elizabeth, had a cousin called Mary, a girl about fifteen years old, who lived in a part of Palestine called Galilee, in a town called Nazareth. People used to marry younger in those days than they do now, and Mary was already engaged to a man called Joseph. Now that I have told you that, you can guess that Elizabeth's cousin was our Blessed

Lady herself. But of course in those days nobody knew she was anyone in particular, unless her mother, Anne, or her father, Joachim, had guessed that their daughter could not be so goldenly good and happy and sinless unless God had special plans for her.

Half a year after Gabriel had been sent to talk to Zachary, God sent him with a message to Mary. When he had come into the room where she was, he said, "Hail, full of grace, the Lord is with thee!"

Our Lady thought, "Who is this shining person and why should he say that to me?" She has heard these words so many times since — whenever we begin a "Hail Mary" — that it seems funny to think she was puzzled and a little bit frightened the first time she heard them.

Gabriel saw what she was thinking, so he went on, "Fear not, Mary, for you have found grace with God. You are going to have a Son, and you are to call Him Jesus. He shall be great and shall be called the Son of the Most High, and the Lord God shall make Him a Great King, and His Kingdom shall have no end."

When our Lady heard this, she said, "How shall this be done?" You see, she was sure that it *could* be done; she just wanted to know *how*, not like Zachary who thought Gabriel might have made a mistake!

Gabriel told her that it would be done by the power of God, and he told her that Elizabeth was to have a son as well. Then Mary said, "Behold the handmaid of the Lord; be it done unto me according to your word."

A handmaid is a servant, and "be it done unto me according to your word" meant that she was ready to do anything God wanted of her.

A Life of Our Lord for Children

After Gabriel had gone, Mary thought it would be good if she went to stay with Elizabeth to help her to get everything ready for her baby when he would arrive. So she set out quickly on a journey up into the hills where Elizabeth lived.

When Mary came to the door of Elizabeth's house and called out a greeting, Elizabeth ran to her cousin and said, "Blessed art thou among women, and blessed is the Fruit of thy womb" — and those are some more words that our Lady has heard a great many times since. They mean, "You are blessed, and so is the Baby you are going to have" — God had let Elizabeth know what the angel had told Mary. Nobody else knew yet.

Our Lady's answer to Elizabeth, although she had not thought it out beforehand, is such a lovely poem that I am putting the whole of it here for you to read and even learn by heart if you would like to. If you don't quite understand all the words, never mind; you can hear what splendid words they are anyway:

> My soul doth
> magnify the Lord
> and my spirit hath
> rejoiced in God my Savior
> because He hath regarded
> the humility of His handmaid.
>
> For behold, from henceforth
> all generations shall call me blessed.
>
> For He that is mighty
> hath done great things to me;
> and holy is His name.

His mercy is from
generation to generations,
to them that fear Him.

He hath showed might in His arm.
He hath scattered the proud
in the conceit of their heart.

He hath put down the mighty
from their seat, and hath
exalted the humble.

He hath filled the hungry
with good things;
and the rich He hath
sent empty away.

He hath received Israel His servant,
being mindful of His mercy:

As He spoke to our fathers,
to Abraham and to his seed forever.

Mary stayed with Elizabeth for three months, and before she went home Elizabeth's son had been born.

All the neighbors came to see the baby, and they talked about what he should be called. Most of them thought he ought to be named Zachary after his father. But Elizabeth said, "No, he is to be called John."

The neighbors all said, "Why John? None of your relations are called that." And then somebody said, "Ask his father."

So they brought writing things to Zachary, who still couldn't speak, and he wrote, "John is his name." And as soon as he had written it, while everybody was still being surprised that he wanted the baby to be called John, Zachary found that he could speak again. He began to praise God aloud, and everybody was more astonished than ever. They went home wondering what kind of a great man the baby would grow into, because God had done so many things to show that he was to be somebody important. But no one except Zachary and Elizabeth guessed how very great a man he would be.

Kings, you know, send heralds before them to let people know they are coming. Well, Zachary's son grew up to be St. John the Baptist, who was the herald of the Great King.

This is the song that Zachary made to thank God for the baby he had been given. Like our Lady's song, it is still sung in her Son's Kingdom:

> Blessed be the Lord God of Israel
> because He hath visited and
> wrought the redemption of His people
> and hath raised up
> a Horn of Salvation to us,
> in the house of David His servant,
>
> As He promised by
> the mouth of His holy prophets,
> who are from the beginning:
>
> Salvation from our enemies,
> and from the hand of all that hate us:
>
> To perform mercy to our fathers,
> and to remember
> His Holy Testament,

That oath, which He swore
to Abraham our father,
that He would grant to us,

That being delivered from
the hand of our enemies,
we may serve Him without fear,

In holiness and justice
before Him, all our days.

And thou, child, shalt be called
the prophet of the Highest:
for thou shalt go before
the face of the Lord
to prepare His ways:

To give knowledge
of salvation to His people,
unto the remission of their sins:

Through the bowels of
the mercy of our God,
in which the Orient
from on high hath visited us:

To enlighten them
that sit in darkness
and in the shadow of death;
to direct our feet into
the way of peace.

After John was named, Mary returned to Nazareth,
and presently Joseph came to take her home with him,
and they lived in his little house behind the carpenter's

shop. They must have been very happy there — St. Joseph working hard making chairs and cupboards and all the things carpenters still make, and our Lady baking and sewing and keeping the house clean and washing the clothes, while she waited for her Baby to be born. But they didn't stay there in peace for long.

You remember I told you in the first part of this book that in those days the Romans ruled over a great part of the world, including Palestine. They were rather a hardhearted sort of people, very good at war and very good at making laws; not so good at being kind. But, before our Lord came, being strong was thought much more important than being kind. Well, at the time we are talking about, the Romans did all the sort of things for Palestine that our own government does for us.

Our Lady and St. Joseph had been living in their little house for only about six months when they heard that the Romans wanted everybody to go to the town their families had come from, to be counted, so that the government might know just how many people there were in Palestine. It was the same kind of thing as what we call "taking a census" nowadays. But in those days you had to go to the town your family used to live in to be counted instead of staying at home and having some-one come to count you. It was called "an enrolling."

St. Joseph's town was Bethlehem because that was King David's town and he was descended from King David. So he and our Lady started off on their journey to Bethlehem and arrived there late in the evening and very tired, especially our Lady.

St. Joseph went to the one little hotel and asked for rooms, but the hotel keeper said there were none left —

Bethlehem was packed full because of all the people who had come to be enrolled. I expect St. Joseph tried to find rooms all over the town after that, but it was no use; there just wasn't any room anywhere.

At last, on the edge of the town, they found a cave that was being used as a stable. Although it wasn't a very nice place to spend the night, it was the best they could find. So St. Joseph made our Lady as comfortable as he could, and they settled down for the night. There was already an ox in the cave, and St. Joseph brought in their own little donkey and tied him at the opposite side of the manger.

That same night, in the fields outside the town, shepherds were looking after their sheep. It wasn't safe to leave the sheep out in the fields all night by themselves; robbers might have stolen them or they might have strayed away. In the middle of the night, an angel (we don't know if it was Gabriel this time) came and stood beside the shepherds.

They were very frightened, even more frightened than people generally are when they see an angel, because in the darkness he looked even more shining and magnificent. The brightness of God shone around the shepherds, too, and it was terrifying. But the angel said, "Fear not, for behold, I bring you good news of great joy that is for the whole world. For tonight a Savior is born to you in Bethlehem, the city of David. You will know Him because He is wrapped in swaddling clothes and lying in a manger."

And suddenly the shepherds saw crowds and crowds of angels, and they were all singing: "Glory to God in the Highest, and on earth peace to men of good will."

After they had gone the shepherds said to each other, "Let's go to Bethlehem and find this Baby."

So they left the sheep to take their chance and hurried off to the town. They found the cave where Joseph and Mary were, and Mary's Son had been born. She had wrapped Him up in swaddling clothes made from her veil and laid Him in the manger.

Swaddling clothes are not used anymore; we put babies into little vests and dresses as soon as they are born. But then people used to wrap them up first of all in pieces of linen that had not been made into proper clothes; and they were called "swaddling clothes."

The manger was much the best place to put a baby born in a stable, wasn't it? Much better than the cold, dirty floor.

So far as we know, the shepherds were the first people to know our Lord was born. Certainly they were His first visitors. Isn't it odd to think of all the crowds in Bethlehem, sound asleep, and of all the other people in the world, asleep too, or going about their business, when the most wonderful thing that had ever happened in the whole world had just happened in a cave in Bethlehem? And nobody knew it except our Lady and St. Joseph and the shepherds and the new Baby, who was God.

When a baby was born in Palestine in those days, his mother and father took him to the Temple in Jerusalem and offered a gift there. If they were rich they took a lamb. If they were poor they took a pair of doves or two young pigeons. Our Lady and St. Joseph were poor, and they took doves.

Now, there was an old man in Jerusalem at that time called Simeon and an old lady, eighty-four years old, called Anna. If you go into a church nowadays when there is no Mass or Benediction or anything going on, you will generally see two or three old men and a few old women who always seem to be there, quietly saying their prayers. Simeon and Anna were like those. They loved God and His Temple, and, as they were too old to be working, they spent nearly all their time there, praying and thinking of God.

God had promised Simeon that he would not die before he had seen the Great King who was to come. So when our Lady and St. Joseph brought Jesus into the Temple, God arranged that Simeon was just coming in as well.

As soon as Simeon saw the Baby, Simeon knew who He was, and going up to our Lady, he very gently took the Infant Jesus into his arms.

This is what he said:

> Now dost Thou
> dismiss Thy servant,
> O Lord, in peace,
> according to Thy word;
>
> Because my eyes
> have seen
> Thy salvation,
> which Thou hast prepared
> before the face of all peoples:
>
> A light to the revelation
> of the Gentiles
> and the glory of
> Thy people, Israel.

Our Lady and St. Joseph wondered who Simeon was and how he knew who the Baby was. But Simeon held up his hand and blessed them, and he said to our Lady:

> Behold, this Child
> is set for the fall
> and for the resurrection
> of many in Israel;
> and for a sign
> which shall be
> contradicted;
> and thy own soul
> a sword shall pierce
> that out of many hearts,
> thoughts may be revealed.

While they stood there, Anna came in, and she knew our Lord, too, and for the rest of her life, she spoke of Him to everyone she met.

After they left Jerusalem our Lady and St. Joseph did not go back to Nazareth but returned to Bethlehem again. Nobody knows why. Perhaps trade was bad in Nazareth and St. Joseph thought there was more chance for a good carpenter to make a living in Bethlehem. Anyhow, that is what they did. Some time later there came wise men from the East to Jerusalem.

In carols and stories, we call them "the Three Kings," but we don't really know if they were kings, or how many of them there were. When they arrived, they went first to see King Herod.

Herod was an odd sort of king. He had no right at all to rule over the Jews, but he had gotten himself made king by the Romans, who were the real government of the country and could have thrown him out if Herod had not done what they told him.

The wise men, of course, did not know about all this, so they went to Herod and asked, "Where is He that is born King of the Jews? For we have seen His star in the East and have come to adore Him."

It must have been a terrible shock to Herod. The last thing he wanted to hear was that a Baby had been born who was the real King of the Jews. He called together the most learned men in Jerusalem and said, "Where will the Christ be born?" For he guessed that if a baby had been born who was king by right, it was sure to be the Great King who was to come. The learned men, who were called Doctors of the Law, said it was written by one of the prophets that Bethlehem was the place.

When Herod had heard this he called the wise men and asked them when they had seen the star, and afterward he sent them on to Bethlehem and told them to come back and tell him when they had found the Baby. He pretended that he wanted to go and adore Him, too.

When the wise men reached Bethlehem, wondering how they were to find the right Baby now they were there, the star they had seen in the East came and stood over one of the houses. So they knew that was the place, and they went straight to the house and found Mary and the Baby there.

They were delighted to have come to the end of their journey (most people think they had been two whole years on the way!) and they knelt down and adored the Baby. Then they gave Him the gifts they had brought: frankincense, gold, and myrrh — all very precious things. Incense is a present for God, gold is a present for a king, and myrrh, which is a kind of medicine, is a present for a man. So you see, they were just the right things to bring because this Baby was God and King and Man.

After they had adored the Baby and given Him their presents, the wise men would have gone back to tell King Herod where the Baby King was, but while they were asleep, God warned them not to, so they started home at once without going near Jerusalem.

When Herod discovered this he was furious, and he did one of the most terrible things a king has ever done, or anybody else for that matter: he ordered his soldiers to go to Bethlehem and kill all the babies who were two years old or less. And the soldiers did.

We call those murdered babies "the Holy Innocents" because although they did not know what it was all about, they were the first people to die for our Lord, and they all went straight to Heaven, just as though they had been grown-up martyrs.

If Herod had not been in such a temper he might have guessed that God would not be defeated so easily.

The night after the wise men left Bethlehem, God had warned Joseph in a dream to take Jesus and Mary away from Bethlehem, and out of Palestine into Egypt, so that He would be safe. Joseph got up in the middle of the night and woke Mary and they set off on their journey at once. Before Herod's soldiers came to Bethlehem they were far away.

Mary and Joseph and Jesus stayed in Egypt until an angel came and told Joseph, while he was asleep, that

Herod was dead. Nobody knows for certain how long afterward that was, but it was very likely about two years. So our Lord, if He was two, or a little less, when they went to Egypt, must have been about four years old when they came back — not a baby anymore, but a little boy.

When they returned to Palestine, they heard that Herod's son, Archelaus, was king now. Joseph was afraid the new king might be the same sort of man as his father, so he took Mary and Jesus to Nazareth, where he started a carpenter's shop again. It must have done quite well this time, for they stayed there until Jesus was grown up.

We do not know anything about what Jesus did from then until He was twelve years old. We only know that as soon as He was old enough, He began to learn to be a carpenter, too. It would be nice to know what games He played and if Elizabeth's son, John, ever came to stay with Him. As his mother was our Lady's cousin, and they were so fond of each other, I expect he did.

Each year, on a special feast day, Mary and Joseph and Jesus went up to the Temple in Jerusalem to keep the feast there, but we don't know anything about their journey, or what they did, until the year when Jesus was twelve. That year a very mysterious thing happened. When the feast day was over, Mary and Joseph set out on their journey home with all the other people who had come from Bethlehem. They thought our Lord was with some of the others, but when they looked for Him toward evening, they found that no one had seen Him at all, all day.

You can imagine how they hurried back to Jerusalem — Jesus was lost! They looked for Him for three days before they found Him. He was in the Temple, talking with the priests and surprising them all because He seemed to know more than they did, although He was only a boy of twelve.

Our Lady ran to Him when she saw Him and said, "Son, why have You done this to us? Your father and I have sought You sorrowing!"

Jesus said, "How is it that you sought me? Didn't you know that I must be about my Father's business?" He was reminding them that it was God who was His Father, not St. Joseph, and that it was God's business, not carpentering, that He must attend to first of all.

I don't think anyone quite understands why our Lord stayed in Jerusalem and went back to the Temple that year. But He was God as well as a boy, and it would be very odd if we did always understand Him.

In fact, if everything our Lord did was perfectly easy to understand, we might begin to wonder if He really was God. In the ordinary way, we don't even understand very well the things God makes. For you know He both made and invented everything in the world from rocks to elephants and electricity — and us. Men can spend the whole of their lives studying any one of the things God has made and still not understand all about it. And yet some people are quite surprised to find that they don't always understand God Himself!

When John, the son of Elizabeth and Zachary, was grown up, he went away from his father's house to live in the wild and lonely desert, quite by himself. Every now and again, God asks somebody to go away from other people like that, so that He can make them holy without being interrupted all the time.

In the desert St. John dressed in the skin of a camel, with no comfortable underclothes under it; and to eat, he had locusts and wild honey. Locusts are like big grasshoppers, and they seem to us very odd things to eat, but some people who live in desert places like Palestine still do eat them, frying them in honey made by wild bees; so it did not seem odd to John.

Presently John came out of the desert to the edge of a great river, the Jordan, that runs through that country.

John used to stand on the river-bank and preach. First a few people came to hear him, and then more, and then more still, until there were crowds all going out to the Jordan to hear him.

What do you think he told them?

He said, "You know what happens to useless fruit trees? They are cut down! Repent of your sins and begin to do good; otherwise you will be like useless trees that are cut down and burned for firewood."

When people asked him what they ought to do, he told them, "Whoever has two coats ought to give one of them to a man who has no coat at all. Whoever has too much food in his house ought to give some of it to a man who has none."

Everybody began to think that John might be the Great King himself. He was so holy, he preached so well, and he had begun to baptize people in the Jordan. This was not our Lord's kind of baptism: People who knew they had done wrong, and that their souls needed washing, came and stood in the Jordan, and John poured water over them.

It was as near as John could get to washing people's souls, and it showed that they knew that their souls needed washing! So John's baptisms were a useful way to prepare people for the sacrament of Baptism which really does wash away every kind of sin and makes us God's own children.

Some of the people who came to hear John preach and saw what he was doing were puzzled. They asked him who he was and why he was baptizing people — was he perhaps the awaited Messiah?

But John said, "No, I am not the Christ. I baptize you with water, but He who shall come after me is greater than I am. He shall baptize you with the Holy Spirit, and I am not worthy to carry His shoes."

A little while after that, Jesus came to John and asked to be baptized.

John said, "I ought to be baptized by You, and are You asking to be baptized by me?"

Jesus answered, "Let it be this way now."

So John baptized Him in the river, and as He came up the bank afterward, praying, the skies were opened, and a dove came flying down to our Lord, and a great voice spoke these words: "This is my beloved Son, in whom I am well pleased."

After that, when John saw our Lord in the desert, he pointed Him out to everyone and told them that He was the Great King who was to come and about the dove and about the voice from Heaven.

But the Holy Spirit led our Lord away into the most desolate part of the desert, where there were no other people, only wild animals. Our Lord stayed there, praying and fasting, for forty whole days. You and I would very likely die if we tried to do that. Jesus didn't, only after the forty days He was very hungry.

Now, the Devil hated our Lord particularly, because our Lord was holy and because the Devil knew that there was something special about Him, although Jesus had not let the Devil find out that He was God.

So when the Devil saw our Lord in the desert, all alone and hungry, he thought, "Ah! Now is the time to win this Man away from God!

He went up to our Lord and said, "If You are the Son of God, command these stones to turn into bread."

Our Lord, who of course knew who the Devil was, and what he was trying to do, said, "Not by bread alone does man live, but by every word that comes from the mouth of God."

He meant that God can keep a man alive without food if He wants to. The Devil saw that trick was no good, so he tried something else.

He took our Lord up to the very top of the Temple in Jerusalem and said, "If You are the Son of God, throw Yourself down, for it is written, 'He has given His angels charge over You, and they will carry You in case You hurt Your foot against a stone.'"

Our Lord said, "It is written again, 'Thou shalt not tempt the Lord thy God.'"

That does not mean that our Lord was telling the Devil that He was God Himself. Our Lord was reminding the Devil that it is not right to ask God to work a miracle just for the fun of seeing whether He will. *Tempt* means "try" or "test."

Then the Devil, who might have had the sense to see it was no use by this time, took our Lord up to the highest peak of a mountain and showed Him all the kingdoms of the world and the glory of them, and he said, "I will give You all these, if You will fall down and adore me."

Imagine the Devil offering God the earth that God had made! When at last he found out who our Lord was, he must have felt very foolish indeed. But he didn't find out then. Our Lord answered him, "Begone, Satan! For it is written, 'The Lord thy God shalt thou adore, and Him only shalt thou serve.'"

Then the Devil saw at last that it was hopeless, and he went away. When he had gone, angels came with food for our Lord, and afterward He went back into the part of the country where St. John was.

Four

The Kingdom of God Is at Hand

Some of the men who went to hear John preach and to be baptized by him had decided to stay with him so that they might learn to be holy and to pray and serve God as he did; they were called his disciples. *Disciple* means "learner."

When John the Baptist saw our Lord coming back to the Jordan again, he turned to his disciples and reminded them of our Lord's baptism and told them again that this was the Man whose way he was preparing. Two of them, who were called Andrew and John, thought that if their master said such things about Jesus they ought to get to know Him if they could. So they followed our Lord along the riverbank when He walked away from John the Baptist. Our Lord turned and saw them and said, "What are you looking for?"

Andrew and John replied, "Master, where do You live?"

And our Lord answered, "Come and see."

So they walked along together to the house where our Lord was staying, and they spent the day there, making friends with Him.

In the evening Andrew went to find his brother, Simon, and he told him, "We have found the Christ," and brought Simon to our Lord. As soon as He saw Simon, Jesus said, "Your name is Simon, but now you shall be called Peter."

Next day our Lord went out again, and He met a man called Philip; He told Philip to come with Him. Philip came, and when he had been a little while with our Lord, he went to find his best friend, Nathaniel, and told him, "We have found the Man who is written about in the Scriptures, and it is Jesus, the Son of the carpenter at Nazareth."

Nathaniel said, "Can anything good come from Nazareth?" I suppose he didn't like Nazareth!

Philip said, "Come and see."

When Jesus saw Nathaniel coming, He said, "Behold an Israelite in whom there is no guile."

That meant that He knew Nathaniel was a good and truthful man. Nathaniel didn't waste time saying, "Oh, I am not good."

He said, "How can You know me?"

And our Lord gave him a mysterious answer, "Before Philip called you, when you were under the fig tree, I saw you."

Nathaniel answered, "Master, You are the Son of God; You are the King of Israel!"

When people called our Lord the "Son of God," they did not mean that they knew He was God the Son, for they did not understand about the Blessed Trinity. Nobody, except our Blessed Lady, knew yet that Jesus was God. "Son of God" was one of the names the Great King was called by the prophets, and it meant no more, so far as anyone knew, than that He behaved to God as a good son behaves to his father.

Our Lord answered Nathaniel, "You shall see greater things than this. You shall see the heavens opened and the angels ascending and descending upon the Son of Man."

"Son of Man" is another name that one of the prophets had used in speaking of the Great King, and it means simply "Man." You or I would not go about calling ourselves "man" or "boy" or "girl," would we? Calling Himself "Son of Man" was one of the ways in which our Lord reminded people of the writings of that prophet. It was also a hint that He was not only man but something more.

These five men, Andrew and John, Simon — whom He called Peter — Philip, and Nathaniel, were our Lord's first disciples. They stayed with Him, when they could, to hear Him preach and to learn all they could from Him. But they did not leave their families and their business for good until later on. Most of them were fishermen, and in between being with Jesus they went home and fished and told their friends about Him.

Soon there were more than five disciples, but the Gospels do not tell us how all of them came to follow our Lord, only these first ones, and some special ones later on.

One day our Lord and the disciples who were with Him were all invited to a wedding party at Cana, which is a town in Galilee. When they arrived, they found our Lady had been invited, too, because Nazareth, where she lived, was not far away. St. Joseph must have died before Jesus started out to found His Kingdom, or he surely would have been there as well. Our Lord and His Mother sat together, of course, and you can imagine how pleased they were to see each other again.

As they sat talking, our Lady saw that something was going wrong, and she soon saw what the trouble was; they had no more wine for the guests! So she turned to her Son and said, "They have no more wine."

Our Lord said, "Woman, what is that to you and to me? My hour is not yet come." That sounds to us like a rude answer, because nowadays nobody calls their mother "woman." But in those days it was the polite way to speak to your mother. The rest of what Jesus said meant, "Need we bother about that? It is not time for me to begin to work miracles yet."

But He must have smiled as He spoke, for our Lady beckoned to the waiters, and when they came she said, "Do whatever He tells you."

In those days, when you went to a party, you found big stone jars of water standing by the door. The water was meant for washing your hands and your dusty feet. Nobody wore shoes and stockings, only sandals, so everybody's feet got dusty and needed washing just as yours do when you wear sandals now.

There were six of these big jars standing near the door of the room where our Lord and our Lady were sitting. Our Lord told the waiters to fill them all full of water. It must have puzzled the waiters to know what good that would do, but they filled them up, just as Jesus said. Then He told them to do something that must have seemed odder still. He said they were to put some of the water in a wine jug and take it to the man in charge of the party, who was called the chief steward. When they brought it to him, he tasted it and thought, "Thank goodness they have found more wine somewhere!"

Our Lord had turned the water into wine! And it was such good wine that the chief steward took the bridegroom aside and scolded him for keeping the best wine until the party was half over! That was our Lord's first miracle, and it is worth remembering that He worked it because His Mother wanted Him to.

After the party, our Lord and our Lady and the disciples all went to Capharnaum for a few days. From there our Lord and His disciples went to Jerusalem, and our Lady went home.

Jesus wanted to be in Jerusalem for a great feast day that was coming. This feast was like what a holy day of obligation is for us.

In those days, you know, there was only one Temple, and only at the Temple could sacrifices of doves and lambs and other things be offered to God. This was part of the plan by which God was preparing the world for our Lord's coming, and I am very glad — aren't you? — that it isn't so anymore. Imagine what it would be like if we all had to go to London or New York to worship God properly at Christmas or Easter!

Now, because animals were killed in the Temple as sacrifices to God, and because so many people came to Jerusalem on feast days, somebody had to sell them doves and lambs and other things to offer in the Temple. And since many Jews came from foreign countries there had to be somebody to change their foreign money into a kind they could use in Jerusalem.

It is just the same nowadays when you go into a new country you have to use a different kind of money. So any that you bring with you has to be exchanged, and there are always people who make it their business to do this for you.

No one could say there was anything wrong with selling doves or changing money outside the Temple. But the merchants and the money changers had grown so bold and cared so little for anything but their trade that they set up a market right inside the Temple!

What would we think if we found a very noisy market inside one of our churches? Well, people had gotten used to the idea and didn't take much notice, but our Lord did.

When He saw what was going on in His Father's house, He made a whip of cords, and with it He drove all those traders out of the Temple, along with their oxen and lambs and all the rest of it. And He turned over the money changers' tables and sent them flying down the steps. He said, "It is written by the prophets, 'My house is a house of prayer'; but you have made it a den of thieves."

When one of the angry crowd asked Him for a sign that He had authority to do such things, He answered, "Destroy this Temple, and in three days I will raise it up again."

"What?" the man shouted. "This Temple took forty-six years to build! And You say You can raise it up in three days after it is destroyed?"

Well, our Lord could have, of course, but really He was giving them the first hint He gave anyone about the Resurrection, when the Temple of His Body was destroyed and in three days He rose again.

It was a little while after this that our Lord heard that St. John the Baptist had been put in prison by Herod. This Herod was one of the sons of the other King Herod, who had tried to kill our Lord when He was a baby, and he seems to have been just as bad as his father. The reason Herod put St. John in prison was this: Herod wanted to have his brother's wife for his own wife, so he took her away from his brother and brought her to the palace to live. Nobody dared to say that he ought not to, except John, who said, "That is against the law."

Herod was furious that John should dare to speak out against him, and so he had put him in prison. Herod wanted to kill St. John as well, but so many people knew John had done nothing wrong that Herod was afraid to kill him without having a good excuse. It was after our Lord heard John was in prison that He began to preach that the kingdom of God was at hand.

This book is meant to tell you something about our Lord's life and especially about how He founded the Kingdom to which we belong. I cannot possibly tell you all the things He said and did, or I would have to write such a big book that you would never want even to begin reading it. So I am not going to tell you all about the man called Nicodemus who came to see our Lord in the middle of the night because he was ashamed to be seen visiting a poor preacher, nor about how our Lord went to Samaria and made friends with a Samaritan woman beside Jacob's well, nor about a little boy He cured in Galilee.

You must read the Gospels themselves for all those stories and a great many more that I have to leave out. The Gospels are four very short books that you can read quite fast: the reason the same story takes so much longer to tell in this book is that the men who wrote the Gospels just went straight on and hardly even stopped to explain anything. They couldn't be expected to know how differently we would live, and that we would have forgotten how people dressed and spoke and built their houses, and the other customs that they had in those days. So I have to stop and explain all the time, but after you have read this book, a good deal of the explaining will have been done, and you can start reading the Gospels anytime you want to.

Well, when Jesus had heard that John was in prison He went through all the little towns in Galilee, preaching and saying, "The kingdom of God is at hand." He preached both outdoors and in the synagogues on the Sabbath Days.

Do you know what a synagogue is? There is very likely one quite near you. It is a sort of Jewish church. You know that the only real church the Jews had was the Temple in Jerusalem. But they couldn't all be going to the Temple every week, so in each little town there was a house set apart as a place to meet and pray in on Saturdays. They called Saturdays "Sabbath Days," and they were the same kind of days for the Jews that Sunday is for us, as I told you at the beginning of this book.

If we couldn't get to Mass on Sunday more than once or twice a year, we wouldn't just do nothing at all about it, would we? We would have a place to meet and say the Rosary and some other prayers on Sundays. Well, that would be the same sort of idea as Jewish synagogues. They were used for schools as well as for churches.

Presently Jesus came to Nazareth and preached in the synagogue there, and I expect our Lady heard Him. From there our Lord went to another town called Capharnaum, and He began to be known as a great Preacher all over that part of the country.

The people who heard Him said that He taught as no one else did. For He did not say, "You ought to do this, because it is written in the Scriptures," but, "You ought to do this, because I say so."

This annoyed the scribes dreadfully. They were people whose work was making copies of the Old Testament by hand, because there was no book printing then. The scribes spent so much time over their copying that they had come to be looked upon as knowing a great deal about Holy Scripture and as having the right to explain what it meant. *The Scriptures* means "the writings" but the word was used to mean the Old Testament, which was the most important collection of writings that they had. *Scribe* really means "writer."

When our Lord went into the synagogue in the town of Capharnaum, there was a man there who was possessed by a devil. In those days devils had much more power than they have now, and they often used to take possession of those who were particularly wicked. When that happened it meant that the possessed person could not speak or move or do anything other than what the devil made him do. When this devil saw Jesus, he made the man he possessed cry out, "Let us alone! Have You come to destroy us? I know who You are, the Holy One of God."

Jesus said to the devil, "Be quiet and go out of him." And the devil went away and left the man perfectly all right again. After that, our Lord was more talked of than ever, for everyone who had seen it was frightened, and they said, "Who can this be? He commands the devils and they obey Him!"

From Capharnaum Jesus went to Peter's house by the Sea of Galilee and there He found that Peter's wife's mother was very ill with a fever. Our Lord went up to her room and took her hand, and all at once she felt quite well again and came downstairs to get their supper.

After the sun went down, when it was cool, all the neighbors brought any sick people they knew of to our Lord to be cured as well, and He cured them all. A great crowd of people came, too, to hear our Lord and to see the people cured.

Very early next morning Jesus got up and went out into a wild part of the country to pray, for He knew the crowds would be back and that there would be no peace once they found Him. Peter and the other disciples went to look for Him. When they came to the place where He was, they said, "Everyone is looking for You."

Our Lord answered them saying, "I must preach the kingdom of God to other towns and cities, for that is what I have come for."

So they set off again through Galilee, our Lord preaching and healing and sending devils away from people who were possessed by them.

The Sea of Galilee, beside which Peter and a lot of our Lord's other disciples lived, is not really a sea at all, but an enormous lake. It is so big that it has waves on it and looks blue, just like a real sea, but it isn't salt. There are all kinds of fish in it, and a great many fishermen live on its shores and make a living by catching fish and selling them.

Peter and Andrew and James and John and a good many of the other disciples were fishermen. Our Lord often walked by the shore of the little sea and taught there, out in the open air.

One day, a great crowd was waiting to hear Him speak. He was standing on the shore, and almost being pushed back into the water because there were so many people who were so eager to get near Him. Looking around, He saw that there were two boats drawn up on the beach nearby. The fishermen they belonged to were washing their fishing nets nearby, and one of them was Peter. Our Lord called to him to take Him out a little way onto the sea in his boat.

When Peter had done that, our Lord sat in the boat and taught the people from there. After He had finished speaking He told Peter to launch out into deep water and let down his net for fish.

Peter said, "Master, we have been out fishing all night and have not caught anything at all, but if You say so, we will try again now."

So they put out their net and immediately caught so many fish that it broke! They had to make signs to their partners, who had gone out fishing in the other boat, to come and help them.

These two were James and John, and they came as fast as they could, and filled both boats with fish until they were almost sinking. When Peter saw this, he knelt down at our Lord's feet and said, "Depart from me, for I am a sinful man, O Lord!"

But our Lord said, "Fear not; from now on you shall catch men." When they had brought the ship to land, Peter and Andrew, James and John, left everything — their houses and their friends and their boats and all those fish! — and they followed our Lord, not just sometimes anymore, but always.

There began now to be such crowds coming to our Lord wherever He was that He thought it better to stay away from the big cities and towns. Out in the open country there were not quite so many people. Even so, crowds gathered wherever He went.

After a while He did go to Capharnaum again, but when the people in the city heard the news that He was there, they all crowded into the house where He was, to hear Him. Among the crowd were some of the Pharisees and learned men of Jerusalem, who were listening to see what they should think of Him.

The Pharisees were people who thought it very important indeed to follow the Law that God had given to Moses, down to the very last little detail. Perhaps that ought to have been a good thing, but since the days of Moses, all sorts of extras had gotten added to the Law. Most of these were fussy things that Moses never intended, and by our Lord's time it was all so very complicated that no one except the Pharisees (who were mostly rich and learned) had time or patience even to try to keep it all exactly.

The Pharisees thought a great deal of themselves for doing this and attending to all these little rules. They were furious if anyone wanted to change any of the things they had been taught to do and were teaching others to do. Altogether, they were remarkably tiresome people, who loved to be seen doing good. They used to give money to beggars and say their prayers where everybody could see them, and so on. And I don't know anything worse than somebody who wants you to admire his holiness all the time, do you?

Well, if these Pharisees had come to see what our Lord was like, they came at a good time. While He was teaching, a party of men carrying a sick man in a bed arrived at the house our Lord was in.

Beds in those days were just thin mattresses, so you could pick a sick man up in his bed and carry him around quite conveniently. But even so, these men could not bring this sick man to our Lord: there were so many people in the house where He was that they could not get through the door!

When they discovered this, they had a very good idea: they took the sick man, still in his bed, up onto the roof. It wasn't the sort of roof our houses have; it was made of dried palm leaves, so it was quite easy to make a hole in it.

They made a very big hole in the roof of the room our Lord was sitting in. (I don't know what the man who owned the house thought of this!) Then they let the sick man in his bed gently down onto the floor so that he lay just in front of Jesus.

Our Lord looked at the sick man and saw that he had been a very wicked man indeed, but that he was sorry now, and that this man had guessed who our Lord was and that our Lord could cure him. Seeing all this, Jesus said, "Be of good heart, son, your sins are forgiven you."

At that all the Doctors of the Law and the Pharisees began to say to each other, "That is a blasphemy! No one can forgive sins except God."

Our Lord knew what they were thinking. He said, "Why do you think evil in your hearts? Is it easier to say, 'Your sins are forgiven,' or to say, 'Arise and walk'?"

Of course, the Doctors of the Law and the Pharisees all thought it was much easier to say, "Your sins are for-given," because you can't see whether people's sins are forgiven or not, but you can see if they are able to walk.

The illness the poor man who had been let down through the roof was suffering from had made him quite helpless, so that he could no more get out of bed than a new baby. But our Lord turned to him and said, "Arise, take up your bed, and walk."

Then He turned back to the other people in the room and said, "I have done this so that you may know that the Son of Man has power on earth to forgive sins."

In the meantime the sick man had jumped out of his bed, rolled it up neatly and walked off with it, just as our Lord had told him to. And as he went he gave thanks to God. The rest of the people did not know whether to be more frightened or astonished, but they also praised God and they said, "We have seen wonderful things today." But I am afraid the Pharisees thought less of the wonder they had seen than of what was to become of them and their teaching if everyone listened to our Lord, and all through the rest of His life they were watching for a chance to put Him in the wrong.

When our Lord and His disciples walked through a wheat field on a Sabbath Day and rubbed the ripe ears of wheat in their hands (have you ever done that?), they said it was wrong because it was really reaping, and that was work and ought not to be done on the Sabbath. And when He healed a man with a withered hand on another Sabbath Day, they said that was work and He ought not to do it on the Sabbath! Did you ever hear such nonsense?

Just after He had cured the man who was let down through the roof, our Lord walked down to the lakeside.

On the way there, He saw a man collecting taxes. The Romans used to tax people just as our government taxes us now, but they had a very odd way of doing it. Instead of collecting the tax money themselves, they gave the job of collecting it in each part of the country to the person who would pay most to be allowed to do it. They told him how much money he must send to the government, but he was allowed to arrange the taxes as he pleased. He could get as much money out of people as he liked and keep what was over for himself! The people who did this collecting, and the clerks who helped them, were called publicans. They were usually very rich, and all the other people hated and despised them, and would not have anything to do with them if they could help it. But when our Lord saw this publican, whose name was Matthew, he said to him, as He had to His first disciples, "Follow me."

And the publican got up and went with our Lord as he was told. He brought our Lord into his own house and made a great feast for Him and invited all his friends. These friends were mostly publicans, too, because nobody wanted to know them or to be seen with them. When the Pharisees heard about this they thought it was another good chance to find fault, so they came to the disciples and said, "Why do you go to dinner with publicans and sinners?"

Our Lord heard and answered for them, "I came not to call good men, but sinners. Those who are well do not need a doctor, but those who are sick do."

The Pharisees had no answer to that, so they said, "Why is it that your disciples don't fast? Ours do, and John's used to."

Our Lord said, "The guests at a wedding can't very well fast while the bridegroom is there, can they? But when the bridegroom goes away they will fast."

He meant that while He was on earth walking and talking with His disciples it was not the time for them to fast, but after He had gone away they would. "The Bridegroom" was another of the names that the prophets used for the Great King.

After this, the Pharisees met together to see if they could find a way to destroy our Lord, and from that time on they plotted against Him.

Five

The Apostles Begin Their Training

One night about this time, our Lord went up into the mountains alone and stayed there all night, praying. In the morning He called His disciples to come up to Him, and from them He chose twelve to be His Apostles.

Disciple, as you remember, means "learner." Well, *apostle* means "someone who is sent." These twelve were the men He chose to be the ones He would send as the first rulers and teachers to spread His Kingdom.

These are their names: Simon, who was called Peter, and Peter's brother Andrew, James and John, Philip and Bartholomew, Matthew and Thomas, another one called James and his brother Jude, another Simon, and Judas Iscariot.

All of these had already begun to be trained for the great work they were to do, but now He kept them with Him and began to teach them more thoroughly so that they might be ready when the time came that He would no longer be with them.

The first great teaching He gave to His disciples after He had chosen the twelve Apostles is called the Sermon on the Mount.

A Life of Our Lord for Children

A great crowd had come looking for Him. He could
see them from where He stood on the mountain. Perhaps
some of them were near enough to hear what He said.
But the sermon was really for the disciples, and for us,
more than for the crowds who did not yet know our Lord.
This is how He began:

> Blessed are the poor in spirit:
> for theirs is the kingdom of Heaven.
>
> Blessed are the meek:
> for they shall possess the land.
>
> Blessed are they that mourn:
> for they shall be comforted.
>
> Blessed are they that
> hunger and thirst after justice:
> for they shall have their fill.
>
> Blessed are the merciful:
> for they shall obtain mercy.
>
> Blessed are the clean of heart:
> for they shall see God.
>
> Blessed are the peacemakers:
> for they shall be called
> the children of God.
>
> Blessed are they that
> suffer persecution for justice' sake:
> for theirs is the kingdom of Heaven.
>
> Blessed are you when they
> revile you and persecute you,

and speak all that is evil
against you, untruly, for my sake:

Be glad and rejoice:
for your reward is very great in Heaven.

Since it is a long sermon I will not tell you all the
other things that are in it — you can read all of it in the
Gospel of St. Matthew, if you like. This is how it ends:

Everyone that hears
these my words and does them
shall be likened to a wise man
that built his house upon a rock.

And the rains fell
and the floods came
and the winds blew
and they beat upon that house,
and it fell not, for it was
founded on a rock.

And everyone that
hears these my words
and doeth them not
shall be like a foolish man
that built his house upon the sand.

And the rains fell
and the floods came
and the winds blew
and they beat upon that house,
and it fell, and great was
the fall thereof.

After that He and His disciples came down from the mountain and went to Capharnaum. In Capharnaum there was a centurion who had a servant who was very ill. (A centurion is a Roman officer with a hundred men under him.) This centurion had heard of our Lord, and when he got news that our Lord was in Capharnaum, he sent some friends of his who were learned and good Jews to meet Him and to ask Him to cure his poor servant.

The Jews who brought his message told our Lord that this centurion was a very good man and had built them a synagogue, although he was a Roman.

Our Lord started to go with them to the centurion's house, but as they were coming near to it another message came that said, "Lord, I am not worthy that You should enter under my roof. Say but the word, and my servant shall be healed. For I also am a man subject to authority, having soldiers at my command, and I say to one, 'Go!' and he goes, and to another, 'Come!' and he comes, and to my servant, 'Do this!' and he does it."

When our Lord had heard this message, He marveled and said to His disciples, "I have not found such great faith, not even in Israel."

The centurion knew that authority comes from above — a captain in the army would have no authority if he were not subject to the officers above him, would he? So he understood that if our Lord could cure diseases and drive out devils He must be doing it subject to God's authority — no one else could have given Him power to order diseases and devils about, as an officer orders his men!

The centurion was a Roman, not a Jew. He did not belong to the Chosen People who had been so carefully prepared for our Lord's coming. Still, he understood and believed our Lord more quickly than the Jews did!

When the centurion's friends got home they found his servant quite well again. I particularly like that sensible centurion, don't you? Our Lord must have liked him especially, too, because all of us, priests and people, repeat the beginning of his message, with only one word changed, every time we go to Holy Communion: "Lord, I am not worthy that Thou shouldst enter under my roof, but say only the word, and my soul shall be healed."

From Capharnaum, our Lord and the disciples went to another city called Naim. When they came near the city they saw a funeral coming toward them. It was a boy's funeral. His body was carried on a bier, which is like a stretcher for dead people, and his mother was following behind it, crying. The boy was her only son, and her husband was dead, so he was all she had to love, and she was very miserable now that he had died. A great crowd of people were following the funeral to show how sorry they were and to try to comfort her.

When our Lord saw all this, He went up to the poor mother and said, "Weep not."

Then He put His hand on the bier, and the men carrying it stood still. He said to the dead boy, "Young man, I say to you, arise!"

And the boy sat up and began to talk, and our Lord picked him up and gave him to his mother. No one is sure just how old he was, but very likely he was quite a little boy. Boys were called young men in those days — after all, they are, aren't they?

This was our Lord's greatest miracle yet, and it was told with fear and wonder all over the countryside.

All this time John the Baptist was still in King Herod's prison, but his disciples used to go and visit him there, and they brought him word of what Jesus was doing. John thought, "It is high time my disciples understood who Jesus is."

So he sent two of them to our Lord with a message, "Are you the Great King who is to come, or are we to look for somebody else?"

They brought the message to Jesus, and our Lord told them to sit near Him and wait a little while for their answer. As they waited many sick people came to our Lord to be cured, and blind men who wanted to see, and people possessed by devils.

Our Lord did everything they wanted. Then He turned to St. John's disciples and said, "Go and tell John what you have seen; the blind see, the lame walk, lepers are made clean, the deaf hear, the dead rise again, the good news is preached to the poor, and blessed is he that is not shocked by what I do."

The messengers went back to John, and surely they were content. When they had gone our Lord began to talk to the crowds about John.

He said, "What did you go out into the desert to see? A reed shaking in the wind? What did you go out to see? A man in beautiful clothes? No, you would have looked for beautiful clothes in a palace, not in a desert. Well, what did you go out to see? A prophet? Yes, and more than a prophet. This is the man of whom it is written in the Scriptures 'I will send my angel before Your face to prepare Your way.' And I say to you that there has never been a greater man than John the Baptist, but lesser men in the kingdom of Heaven shall be greater than he."

Everyone who had been baptized by John was glad to hear our Lord praise him, but the Pharisees who had refused to have anything to do with him were not pleased at all.

It was now that our Lord began to teach in parables. *Parable* is the name for a particular kind of story, and it comes from a Greek word that means "to put alongside." So in our Lord's parables two meanings are put alongside each other. One is a simple meaning that you understand at once, and the other is something our Lord wanted to teach.

Generally the people in the crowds He preached to didn't know what the second meaning was. But no one forgets a good story. So when the Apostles were sent out to preach much later on, they could remind people of the parables, and explain what they meant. Or people who thought carefully about them might guess the meaning by themselves.

The reason our Lord taught in parables instead of telling everybody straight out just what He meant is the same reason that children in school don't have the same lessons as students in college: they are not ready for anything so difficult yet.

The crowds listening to our Lord were not ready to hear all He had to tell them. They had to learn very gradually, and the parables were the best first step and gave them something to think about, because everyone knew there was a second meaning, even when they couldn't guess what it was.

Here is a parable that our Lord told when He was standing on the seashore one morning:

"One day a man went out to sow seed for a farmer, and as he sowed, some of the seed fell by the roadside and was trodden on by the people passing by, and birds came and ate it. Some fell upon rocky ground and as soon as it had begun to grow, it withered away because there was not enough water there for it. Some fell among brambles, and the brambles grew faster than the seed and choked it. But some fell upon good ground and when it had grown up it made seed in its turn, and gave the farmer thirty or sixty or a hundred seeds for every one he had sown."

When the crowds had left Him after this sermon, the twelve Apostles came to Him and asked Him what it meant.

Our Lord said, "To you it is given to know the mysteries of the kingdom of God, but I teach the rest in parables, so that they see without seeing and hear without really understanding."

Our Lord wanted the people in His crowds to understand, but He knew it was better for them to hear the story and understand only the easy meaning than not to hear it at all. But, because the Apostles were

staying with Him to learn, and were being prepared for their work in the Kingdom, He told them a great deal more than He told anyone else.

This is the way He explained the parable about the man who went out to sow seed:

"The seed," He said, "is the word of God. What happened to the seed that fell by the road is what happens when people who have heard me speak allow the Devil to come and take the word out of their hearts. What happens to the seed that fell on rocky soil is like what happens when people hear my word with joy but fall away when they are tempted. What happens to the seed that fell among brambles is like what happens to people who hear my teaching and believe it, but have so many cares and riches and pleasures of their own that all these things choke the teaching and it cannot grow.

"But the seed that falls on good ground and so brings forth good

grain is like what happens when a man hears my words and keeps them in a good and perfect heart."

I cannot tell you all of our Lord's parables, but here is one more that He explained afterward to the Apostles. It is all about the Kingdom, as most of the parables are. This one also begins with a man sowing seed. Some people think that from where our Lord stood on the seashore He could see the farmers sowing or reaping, according to the time of year, and that is one reason the parables are full of country things of that sort. They are lovely things to read about anyway.

"The kingdom of Heaven is like this. A man sowed good wheat in his fields, but while he was asleep, an enemy came and oversowed weeds among it, and went away. When the wheat began to grow, the weeds began to grow, too. The farmer's men came to him and said, 'Sir, did you not sow good seed in your field? How is it that it is full of weeds?' The farmer said, 'An enemy has done this.' The men said, 'Shall we go and pull the weeds up?' But the farmer said, 'No, because perhaps in rooting out the weeds, you will root out the wheat as well. Let them both grow until the harvest, and then I will tell the reapers to gather the weeds first and bind them into bundles to burn, but the wheat is to be gathered into my barn.' "

This is the way our Lord explained this parable to His Apostles: "The man who sowed the good seed is the Son of Man. And the field is the world, and the good seed are the children of the Kingdom, but the bad seed are the children of the Devil. The harvest is the end of the world, and the reapers are the angels. As the weeds are gathered up and burned in the fire, so shall it be at the end of the world. The Son of Man shall send His angels and they shall gather out of His Kingdom all wicked and evil men and throw them into the fire. Then shall good men shine like the sun in the kingdom of their Father."

There is a parable, too, about the kingdom of Heaven being like buried treasure, and there is one about it being like a net full of good and bad fish and there is another in which our Lord says it is like a mustard tree that starts as the tiniest of seeds and grows into a great tree with birds in its branches. And there are many more as well, which you can find in the New Testament and read for yourselves. After He had told these parables our Lord said to His Apostles, "Have you understood all these things?"

When they said, "Yes," He told them, "Every scribe instructed in the kingdom of Heaven is like a man who is a householder, who brings forth out of his treasures new things and old."

One day our Lord said to His Apostles, "Let us cross the sea."

So they all got into a boat and set off across the little Sea of Galilee. It is big enough to be very rough, even if it is only really a great lake. Our Lord was tired out with all the preaching and curing He had done that day, and He fell fast asleep in the bow of the boat with a cushion under His head.

They sailed along quite peacefully for a while, and then a storm came up, as bad as a storm on a big sea. Great waves broke over the boat and began to fill it with water, so that it was in danger of sinking, but Jesus was so tired that He still slept on.

When the Apostles could reach Him they woke Him up and said, "Master, the ship is going to sink, and we shall all be drowned."

Our Lord stood up and told the wind and the sea to be quiet, and a great calm fell. Then He said to His Apostles, "Where is your faith? Did you really think I would let you drown?"

But they were almost more afraid at the sudden calm than they had been at the danger of drowning, and they said to each other, "Who can this be that the winds and the sea obey Him?"

You see, they still didn't really understand that our Lord was God. If they had, they would have been too frightened to have treated Him as a friend. That was why He let them find out only little by little, after they knew Him well enough not to be too much afraid of sitting and talking with Him, even if He was God.

When they landed on the other side of the sea they were in the country of the Gerasenes. There a very miserable man met them. I expect it was because of him that our Lord had wanted to go there. This man was possessed by a devil, and had been for a long time. He lived alone in a graveyard, and he wore no clothes. When Jesus saw him He told the devil to go out of him. But the devil made the man fall down on his face and cry in a loud voice, "What have I to do with You, Jesus, Son of the Most High God? Do not torment me."

Our Lord said, "What is your name?"

And the devil answered, "Legion." That means "a great many," for there was not just one devil possessing the poor man, but a whole crowd of them. And they asked our Lord not to send them straight back to Hell

but to let them instead go into a herd of pigs that was feeding nearby. Our Lord told them they might. So they went out of the man and into the pigs, and the whole herd rushed frantically down a steep bank into the sea and were drowned. The men in charge of the pigs were terrified when they saw this and ran home to tell others what had happened.

When they had heard the news, all sorts of people from the towns and villages round about came to see our Lord, and they found the man who had been possessed so long by so many devils, sitting on the ground beside Jesus, sane and properly dressed.

You would think they would have welcomed our Lord, but they seem to have thought more of pigs than of men, for they all asked Him to please go away. So our Lord went down to the boat again with the Apostles.

The man who had been possessed asked to come with them and to be allowed to be with our Lord always. But Jesus told him that what he must do was to return to his own home and there tell what had been done for him. So he did that, and got his part of the country all ready for the Apostles when they began to spread the gospel of the Kingdom later on.

When they got back to Galilee, the crowds were waiting for our Lord by the seashore. He had no sooner landed than a man called Jairus came pushing his way through the crowd. When Jairus reached our Lord he knelt down at His feet and asked Him to please come to his house because his daughter was dying and only Jesus could save her.

Our Lord went with him at once. And as they were going through the crowd a woman who had been very ill for twelve years came close to our Lord. She had been to all kinds of doctors, and none of them had done her any good at all, but she was sure that our Lord could cure her. When this woman found herself close behind our Lord she thought to herself, "If I can just touch the hem of His garment, I shall be well again." So she put out her hand and touched His garment, and at once she was perfectly well.

But our Lord stood still and said, "Who touched my clothes?"

The disciples said, "Why, the crowds are pressing on us all from every side! How can You ask who touched You!"

Our Lord answered, "Somebody did touch me." And He looked around to see who it was.

The poor woman was frightened and wondered if she had been too bold, but she came forward and knelt at our Lord's feet, and told Him all about it. Our Lord said, "Your faith has made you well. Go in peace."

While this was happening a messenger came from Jairus's house and told him not to bother Jesus any further because his daughter had just died.

But our Lord said to Jairus, "Fear not, only believe."

When they came to the house, He would not let anyone go into the little girl's room except Peter and James and John and her father and mother.

The house was full of people mourning and crying aloud; we like to be very quiet and not have a crowd of people making a noise in the house when anyone dies, but in those days a great deal of noisy crying was the custom. Our Lord said to all these people, "Why are you making such a to-do, and crying so? The maiden is not dead; she is asleep."

They laughed at Him very scornfully, because they were quite sure they knew the difference between death and sleep, and that the little girl was dead. But when He came into her room, He took her by the hand and said, "Little maid, arise."

The little girl sat up at once, and Jesus gave her to her parents and told them to be sure to give her something to eat. He told them, too, not to say anything about what He had done, but they could hardly help it, for everyone knew that she had been dead, and now she was both alive and well again.

When He left Jairus's house our Lord went home to Nazareth, to see our Lady, I expect. She must have been lonely there now that St. Joseph was dead and our Lord was away preaching.

On the Sabbath Day He went into the synagogue to preach, as you remember He had done once before. But this time He had become so famous that the people of Nazareth could not believe it possible that a boy who had grown up among them could really be able to do all the things they had heard of Him doing.

So they said to each other in the synagogue, "Isn't this Joseph and Mary's Son? The young carpenter who used to live and work here, before He took to all this preaching? Why, we know His brothers, Simon, Jude, and James, and there is nothing special about them!"

Some people have thought that our Lady must have had other children besides our Lord, because of these "brothers." But we know He was her only child, and that Simon, Jude, and James were His cousins. In the language spoken in Palestine then there was no word for *cousin*, and everybody called their cousins brothers and sisters. If you wanted to explain exactly what relation one of your cousins was, you had to say "my father's sister's son" or "my mother's brother's daughter," or whatever it was, and of course that was much too awkward for everyday use.

Our Lord knew what everyone in the synagogue was whispering about, so He said, "Doubtless you will say to me, 'As great things as we have heard of You doing in Capharnaum, do here in Your own country.' But a prophet is without honor in his own country." And He reminded them of two stories from the Old Testament about prophets who had been sent to faraway countries by God, because their own countries would not listen to them.

When the people in the synagogue heard this they were furious, and they drove Jesus out of the city and up to the top of the hill it was built on. They meant to kill Him by throwing Him over a cliff. But it was not time for our Lord to die yet, so He went straight through the crowd as if they were not there, and away from the place where He had been brought up, for the last time.

If they had let Him stay, His miracles might have shown them that He was more than just an upstart carpenter, but they were in such a hurry to send Him away that there was no time for miracles.

⇛

Now comes a great moment in the founding of the Kingdom: our Lord called His Apostles to Him and gave them power and authority over devils and over diseases, and He sent them to preach the kingdom of God. This was the first time the Apostles had been sent to preach.

Before, they had always listened to our Lord and perhaps tried to answer the questions of people in the crowd round about. Now they were to preach themselves and cast out devils and cure sickness, just as they had seen our Lord do.

He told them not to go to any country but their own, and that they were to take nothing for their travels, neither food nor money, and that they were to go and stay with people in each city they came to.

They were to preach there in the synagogues and outdoors until it was time to go on to the next city. But everywhere they went they were to say, "The kingdom of God is at hand."

When they had set out, our Lord went preaching again with only the disciples to be with Him, until the Apostles returned.

In the meantime, who do you think was having a birthday, and a great party to celebrate it? King Herod! And John the Baptist was still in prison because he had said that Herod had no right to take Herodias, his brother's wife, away from her husband. Herod had taken her because he wanted her to live in the palace with him.

Now Herodias, even more than Herod, wished John the Baptist was out of the way for good and all, for she was always afraid that he would make Herod send her home. Now that she was a queen in a palace, she did not at all want to go back to her own husband again. Because of this she was always plotting to have John killed, and when Herod's birthday party was being planned, she thought of a new plot.

She had a little daughter called Salome, who was a wonderful dancer, and after Herod and his guests had finished supper, she sent Salome into the dining room to dance for them.

When Salome had finished dancing, Herod called out, like a king in a fairy tale, that he would give her anything she asked for, even up to half his kingdom. Salome ran to her mother and said, "What shall I ask for?"

And Herodias told her, "Ask for John the Baptist's head on a dish."

So Salome, who, I hope, didn't quite know what it would mean, came back and asked for that.

Herod was sad, or pretended to be, but he had promised, so he sent soldiers to cut off John's head there and then, and it was brought to Salome on a dish, just as she had asked.

But if Herod thought he would be in peace now that John was dead, he was wrong. Jerusalem was full of rumors about our Lord and His miracles. Herod heard some of these stories and he thought, "This is John the Baptist again — I beheaded him, and now he has risen from the dead, and it is all worse than ever!"

Six

Who the King Is

When the Apostles came back to our Lord after their preaching and healing expedition, they told Him all about it and everything they had done. Our Lord listened to it all, and then He said, "Come into a quiet country place with me, and we will rest a little."

You see, the crowds were all around our Lord still, and they wanted so much attention that there was not even time to sit down and have a proper meal. So they took their boat and sailed away across the Sea of Galilee again. On the other side of the sea they climbed up onto a mountain, so as to have a little peace and quiet for once.

But the people who saw them set out in their boat guessed where they were going, and followed as fast as they could, so that our Lord and the Apostles cannot have had much time to rest before there were as many people climbing up the mountain to them as they had left on the other side of the sea.

When our Lord saw that they had come so far to find Him again, He was sorry for them. He forgot about being so tired and began to teach them and heal the sick people they had brought with them.

In the evening there were still thousands of people up in the mountain, far away from their homes, or indeed, from any houses at all. When the Apostles saw how late it was getting they asked our Lord to send everybody away, while there was still time for them to buy themselves some food for supper when they got back to the towns and villages near the foot of the mountain.

But our Lord said, "There is no need for them to go. You give them food for their supper."

Philip replied, "It would take far more money than we have to buy them even a taste of food each!"

I think the Apostles thought our Lord was joking, for Andrew, Peter's brother, said next, "There is a boy here who has five loaves and two fishes, but what use would those be among so many?"

But our Lord was not joking, and He said, "Make everyone sit down in groups of fifty people each." So they all sat down on the green grass and waited to see what would happen next.

They saw our Lord bless the food and then take up one of the loaves and break it, and give the pieces to the Apostles. And He did the same with the fish. When each of the Apostles had as many helpings of bread and fish as he could carry, they took them to the people sitting on the grass.

Then they came back to see if any food was left. It must have puzzled them to see our Lord beginning to feed all those people with a little food that would have been just about enough for Himself and them!

But when they came back to Him they found that there was plenty more bread and fish and so it went on. There seemed to be simply no end to those five loaves and two fishes! At last everyone had eaten all they wanted, although there were five thousand men there, besides a great many more women and children.

Then our Lord told the Apostles to pick up the remains and put it into the baskets so that it should not be wasted. They picked up twelve baskets full, and some of this, I suppose, was what they had for supper.

When the five thousand men understood what our Lord had done for them, they were sure that He was the Messiah, and they decided among themselves to take Him by force and make Him their king. But He did not want to be king of the kind of kingdom they hoped for.

First He told the Apostles to go back to the seashore and start out in the boat at once, and that He would follow them after He had sent the crowds away. I expect the Apostles were as excited as anybody, and as willing to try to make Him king! But they did as they were told, and when they had gone, our Lord made the crowds go away, too, and then went off by Himself, further up the mountain, to pray.

Meantime, in the boat, the Apostles were having a hard time. There was a strong wind against them and they were rowing as hard as ever they could without getting ahead much.

About three o'clock in the morning they saw Jesus walking across the sea toward the ship, with nothing under His feet except the angry waves! They were all frightened, and thought they were seeing a ghost, and cried out. As soon as our Lord heard them He called to them, "It is I! Don't be afraid!"

Peter answered, "Lord, if it is really You, tell me to come to You, walking on the sea as You are."

And our Lord said to Peter, "Come!"

Peter walked straight out of the boat, and went toward our Lord, walking on the top of the waves. I think it was

wonderfully brave of him, don't you? But he couldn't keep on being quite as brave as that. When he felt how strong the wind was he began to be frightened and he called out, "Lord, save me!"

Our Lord caught hold of his hand and said, "O you of little faith! Why did you doubt?"

Then together our Lord and Peter walked the rest of the way to the boat. As soon as they reached the boat the wind died down, and the sea grew calm.

The Apostles came to our Lord then, and adored Him. And they said, "Indeed You are the Son of God." But they still didn't quite know how much that meant.

Early next morning they landed on the shore on the other side of the sea. Everybody recognized our Lord and went rushing to fetch every sick person they knew of, so that He might cure them.

In the meantime, the people He had left on the opposite shore were looking everywhere for Him. They knew He had not set out in the boat with His Apostles, and they knew that no other boat had crossed the sea from anywhere nearby.

Presently ships arrived there with people in them who said that they had seen our Lord on the other side only that morning.

This puzzled them more than ever, but as many as could crossed over themselves, and when they found Jesus they said, "Master, how did You get here?"

Jesus said, "You did not come looking for me because you have seen me do miracles, but because I have given you food. Do not work so hard for the kind of food that goes bad and is of no more use, but work for the food that lasts to life everlasting, which the Son of Man will give you."

They answered, "What shall we do? How shall we work for God?"

This is what our Lord told them: "This is the way to work for God: Believe in Him whom He has sent."

The crowds answered, "What miracle will You do for us to see, so that we may believe in You? Our forefathers were fed with manna in the desert, as we have read in the Scriptures: 'He gave them bread from Heaven to eat.'"

Weren't they a greedy lot? Our Lord had worked a great miracle to feed them just the day before, and now they were asking for another miracle, and hinting that they liked best the sort that gave them a good meal for nothing! ("Manna" was the food that God provided for the Israelites in their journey through the desert where there was nothing else to eat.)

Our Lord said, "What Moses gave your forefathers to eat in the desert was not really bread from Heaven, but my Father will give you the true bread from Heaven which gives life to the world."

When they heard that they said, "Give us always this bread!" But the next thing our Lord said shocked and puzzled them: "I am the bread of life: he who comes to me shall never be hungry, and he who believes in me shall never be thirsty."

The people He was talking to had never heard anything in the least like that, and they began to say to each other, "Isn't this Jesus, the Son of Joseph and Mary? How can He say He came down from Heaven?"

But our Lord, because He had really meant what He said, told them the same thing again, but making it clearer still: "I am the bread of life. Your forefathers ate manna in the desert, and they are dead. I am the living bread that came down from Heaven. If any man eats this bread, he shall live forever."

The people listening to Him were more puzzled than ever, and they were shocked, too. They began to say, "How can this Man give us His flesh to eat?"

So our Lord explained still more clearly: "Unless you eat the flesh of the Son of Man and drink His blood, you shall not have life in you. He that eats my flesh and drinks my blood has everlasting life, and I will raise him up at the last day. For my flesh is food indeed, and my blood is drink indeed. A man who eats my flesh and drinks my blood lives in me, and I live in him. This is the bread that came down from Heaven. Not the sort of food your forefathers ate, and afterward died; he who eats this bread shall live forever."

When the people hearing this really understood that He meant what He said, many of them, even some of His own disciples, went away and would have no more to do with Him.

Our Lord watched them go. Then he turned to His Apostles and said, "Are you going away, too?"

But Peter answered for them all: "Lord, to whom should we go? You have the words of eternal life. And we have believed and known that You are the Christ, the Son of God."

It is very easy for us to say that the disciples who would have no more to do with our Lord after they had heard this teaching were silly, but if we did not know about Holy Communion, it would sound just as surprising to us. No one had heard of anything of the kind in those days, not even from our Lord, so it is no wonder they were puzzled. Only our Lord had done so much to show His power that they ought to have tried harder to believe and understand.

Anyhow, I think we are very lucky to live now, and to have fed our souls on our Lord ever since we were five or six, and quite understood about it.

Did you know that *Bethlehem*, the name of the town where our Lord was born, means "House of Bread"?

The next thing the Pharisees complained about was the way our Lord's disciples sat down to eat without washing their hands first. Of course it is a good plan to wash your hands before dinner, but it isn't a sin not to, is it? Unless you have been told to, and then it is a sin of disobedience, not a sin of not washing your hands! But for a long time the Pharisees had been teaching that it was really wrong.

Our Lord told the Pharisees, when He heard about this, that it was the evil a man had in his heart that made him look dirty to God, not eating without washing first.

About this time He went to two cities outside Palestine called Tyre and Sidon, but I am not going to tell you about what He did there or about the deaf and dumb man He cured on His way home again.

I have to skip some things, as I said before, and you can find both of these stories in the New Testament yourselves.

While Jesus was on His way home from a place called Decapolis, where there are ten cities, another great crowd followed Him. This time again it seemed as if they would have no supper at all if He sent them away. So for the second time He fed them all, this time with seven loaves and a few little fishes, and this time the Apostles picked up seven baskets of scraps afterward.

The next city He came to was Dalmanutha, and from there they sailed for Bethsaida, and there a blind man was brought to our Lord, as soon as He had landed. Jesus took him by the hand and led him aside, out of the town. Then He put spittle from His mouth on the man's eyes and asked him if he saw anything.

The blind man looked up and said, "I see men who look like trees walking." I think he was just trying to do his best, but really couldn't see at all yet! Then our Lord laid His hands on his eyes, and he began really to see, and in a moment saw everything clearly.

Our Lord told him to go home, and if he went into the town not to tell anybody what had happened to him.

Now comes a very important thing. Our Lord and the Apostles went next to a town called Caesarea Philippi. As they were walking along toward it, He asked them who people said He was.

The Apostles gave Him all kinds of answers, for there were all kinds of stories about who Jesus was. Some people said He was the Prophet Elijah come back to earth again, and some that He was John the Baptist risen from the dead, and some that He was the prophet

Jeremiah, or one of the other prophets of Israel. Our Lord listened to all this. Then He said, "But who do you say that I am?"

St. Peter answered for them all, and this is what he said: "Thou art the Christ, the Son of the living God!"

He really understood what Son of God meant, too, for our Lord answered, "Blessed art thou, Simon Bar-Jona, for flesh and blood have not revealed it to thee, but my Father who is in Heaven." He meant, "I did not tell you, so God the Father must have." *Simon Bar-Jona* means "Simon, the son of John"; you remember Peter was called Simon until our Lord changed his name.

Jesus went on:

> And I say to thee:
> that thou art Peter;
> and upon this rock
> I will build my Church,
> and the gates of Hell
> shall not prevail against it.
>
> And to thee will I give the keys
> of the kingdom of Heaven.
>
> And whatsoever thou
> shalt bind on earth,
> shall be bound also in Heaven;
>
> And whatsoever thou
> shalt loose on earth
> shall be loosed also in Heaven.

In the language our Lord was speaking *Peter* and *rock* are the same word, so what He had said sounded like, "I say to you that you are rock, and upon this rock I will build my Church."

Do you remember about the man who built his house upon a rock, "and the floods came and the winds blew and it fell not, because it was founded on a rock"? Well, St. Peter is the rock on which the Church, which is also the kingdom of God, is founded. Nothing can move it or sweep it away; it is perfectly safe until the end of the world. And St. Peter was given authority to let people into the Kingdom or shut them out. That is what our Lord meant by, "To thee will I give the keys of the kingdom of Heaven," and "Whatsoever thou shalt bind on earth shall be bound also in Heaven; and whatsoever thou shalt loose on earth shall be loosed also in Heaven" meant that he was to have authority over the whole Kingdom.

So St. Peter was being made very important, wasn't he? He was to be the first head of our Lord's Church on earth. After he died someone else was chosen to go on doing those things for the Church, and after he died someone else again — and you know who is doing it now: Pope John Paul II. St. Peter was the first pope, and there have been popes ever since — two hundred sixty-four of them altogether!

Our Lord told His Apostles not to tell who He was yet, and He told them why they were not to. He said, "The Son of Man must first suffer many things and be put to death by the scribes and high priests, and the third day after He is killed, He will rise again."

This was the first time our Lord had said anything about how He was to die. Peter, who was feeling very pleased, and perhaps a little bit proud because he was to be head of our Lord's Kingdom, did not like the idea of our Lord being killed at all.

He took Jesus aside and said, "Lord, do not think of such things! Surely nothing of the sort shall happen!"

But our Lord turned on him and said, "Go behind me, Satan! You do not understand the things of God, but only the things of men!"

Poor Peter! He had been so happy and had thought he was doing so well. "Satan" does not mean that our Lord was calling him names, though. We call the Devil Satan, because it means tempter, and the Devil tempts us to do wrong. But it was bad enough to have our Lord calling him a tempter, wasn't it? It sounds very surprising that our Lord, who was so patient with the Apostles as a rule, should have been so suddenly angry with him. But we can understand it, for we know what terrible sufferings our Lord was facing, and that He Himself prayed to be let off them later on.

This is what our Lord said next:

> If any man will come after me,
> let him deny himself
> and take up his cross daily
> and follow me.
>
> For he that will save his life,
> shall lose it;
> and he that shall
> lose his life for my sake,
> shall save it.
>
> For what shall it profit a man
> if he gain the whole world

and suffer the loss
of his own soul?

For he that is ashamed
of me and of my words,
of him the Son of Man
shall be ashamed when
He shall come in His majesty
and that of His Father
and of the holy angels.

I say to you:
there are some standing here
who shall not taste death
until they see the kingdom of God.

About a week after this, our Lord took Peter, James, and John up onto a mountain. Very important things were apt to happen, as I expect you have noticed, when He went up onto a mountain. This time, our Lord began to pray. As He prayed, His face began to look different, and His clothes became white and shining with light. And the Apostles saw two men walking with our Lord, and knew that these men were Moses and Elijah, two of the greatest prophets. Moses and Elijah walked with our Lord and spoke of His death. Peter and James and John felt as if they were dreaming, and Peter heard himself say, "Lord, it is good for us to be here. Let us make three tents: one for You, one for Moses, and one for Elijah."

But while Peter was still speaking a bright cloud covered our Lord and the two prophets, and the Apostles heard a great voice say, "This is my beloved Son: hear Him."

When they heard that voice and saw the strange, shining cloud, they were terrified and fell down on their faces. But in a moment they felt our Lord touch them, and He said, "Arise, and fear not."

They got up and looked all around them then, but there was no one to be seen anymore, except our Lord, and He looked just as usual.

That happening is called the *Transfiguration*, which means the "changing," because Peter and James and John were allowed to see our Lord, just for a few minutes, as we shall see Him in Heaven — not looking like a village carpenter anymore, but even more splendid than they had expected the Great King to look.

As they came down from the mountain, our Lord told them not to tell anyone what they had seen until He had risen from the dead. They wondered what He could mean by that, but they did not like to ask Him.

At the foot of the mountain, a crowd met them. In the crowd was a man whose son was possessed by a devil, an especially bad one that our Lord's disciples had not been able to do anything with. But our Lord sent the devil away.

From there they went through Galilee to Capharnaum again, and stayed for a time in somebody's house there. When they had arrived at Capharnaum Jesus asked the Apostles what they had been talking about on the journey. The Apostles did not know what to say, because they had been quarreling about which of them would be the greatest in the kingdom of God!

You see, the Apostles still thought it was going to be a kingdom like the one Solomon had, and that they would all have very grand positions in the government!

Of course, our Lord knew what they had been doing without their telling Him. He sat down and called a child, who lived in the house where they were staying, to come to Him.

When the child came, our Lord kissed him, and stood him among the Apostles. "Unless you become like little children," He said, "you shall not enter into the kingdom of Heaven. And whoever shall give one of these little ones even a cup of cold water to drink, in my name, shall have a reward. But it would be better for a man to have a great stone tied around his neck and to be thrown into the sea, than that he should teach one of these children who believe in me to do wrong. See that you do not despise these little ones, for their angels always see the face of my Father in Heaven."

And so our guardian angels do, don't they?

Our Lord went on: "If your brother does something to hurt you, speak to him about it by yourselves. And if he will listen to you, then you will be friends again. But if he will not listen, then take two or three others with you and go to him, and perhaps he will listen to them. And if he will not, tell the Church. If he will not listen to the Church, count your brother no more important to you than a heathen or a publican."

After that He gave all His Apostles, who were the beginning of the Church He was talking of, a power He had already given to St. Peter separately: the power of binding and loosing — or unbinding — that is, the power to make laws for His Church. Peter had this power as head of the Church, and the other eleven had it with him as a group, "between them" because they were the first bishops.

This time He added something else: "If two of you shall agree on earth about anything they want to ask my Father for, it shall be done for them by my Father who is in Heaven. For where two or three are gathered together in my name, there am I in the midst of them."

From Capharnaum Jesus went to Jerusalem for one of the great feasts of the Jewish year, called the Feast of Tabernacles. During the holy days, while the feast was going on, our Lord taught in the Temple, and the Pharisees listened and longed more than ever to put an end to Him and His teaching. But so far they could not find a good enough excuse.

Early one morning, when Jesus had come to the Temple and was sitting teaching the people there, the scribes and Pharisees arrived in a crowd. In the middle of the crowd was a woman whom they were holding on to as if she were a prisoner. They stood her before our Lord and told Him she was so wicked and had sinned so badly that by the law of Moses she ought to be stoned. Being stoned meant having large stones thrown at you until your bones were all broken and you died.

The Pharisees thought this a splendid idea for catching our Lord. If He said, "Then why don't you stone her?" they could tell the Romans, who would not let the Jews put anyone to death now that they were ruling the country. But if our Lord said, "Well, I don't think she ought to be put to death," then they could say that He was contradicting Moses!

Our Lord didn't say anything at all to begin with. He stooped over and wrote with His finger on the ground. That is the only time we know of that our Lord wrote anything, and nobody knows what it was. The

Pharisees were not interested in it, anyway. They kept asking, "What are we to do with this woman?"

Presently our Lord straightened up and said, "Let any man among you who has never sinned be the first to throw a stone at her." Then He bent over and went on writing.

The scribes and Pharisees stood there silently for a moment. Then the eldest of them turned away and quietly went out of the Temple, and the rest followed him one by one, until there was no one left in the Temple except our Lord and the woman who had been so wicked. When they were all gone, our Lord lifted Himself up again and looked at her. "Where are the men who accused you?" He said. "Has no one condemned you?"

The woman answered, "No one, Lord."

And our Lord said, "Neither will I condemn you. Go now, and sin no more."

That was one of the many traps the Pharisees laid for our Lord. They were determined to catch Him saying or doing something that they could report either to the Romans or to the Jewish authorities and so turn them against Him.

On one of these occasions He told them that He knew very well what they were trying to do. Of course that made them angrier than ever! While they were still so angry He told them something they had not heard before, "If any man keeps my words, he shall not see death forever."

That was another way of saying that such a man's soul would never die because he would live happily in Heaven forever. But they supposed He meant that He could prevent people's bodies from dying. They thought that was nonsense, so one of them said, "Now we know You are possessed by a devil! Are You greater than Abraham? He died! Who are You claiming to be?"

Our Lord answered, "Abraham rejoiced when I was born; he rejoiced and was glad."

And the Pharisee said, "Have You seen Abraham? Why, You are not even fifty years old yet!"

Our Lord answered with these wonderful and frightening words, "Before Abraham was, *I am.*"

They understood very well what He meant then, for as God had told Moses long ago, the name of God is "*I am who am.*" It is a way of speaking which shows that there is no yesterday and no tomorrow for God, only "now." This is too hard for us really to understand, but we can know about it, and guess a little what it means.

The Pharisees knew, at least, what He was claiming, for they were so furious that they took up stones to throw at Him, so as to kill Him, as they had wanted to kill the wicked woman. But it was not time for our Lord to die yet, so He hid Himself and went out of the Temple, without anybody being able to say how He had gone, or where He was.

While our Lord was still in Jerusalem, He and His disciples were passing by the Temple one day, and they saw a beggar sitting and begging, and he was blind. One of the disciples asked our Lord, "Did this man sin, or his parents?"

They were puzzled, because they thought being blind was a punishment, and they wondered who was being punished — surely not the man who had been blind ever since he was born.

Our Lord said, "It was not because of a sin, but so that God's power should be shown by what I will do for him. As long as I am in the world, I am the light of the world." And He made clay with spittle from His mouth and dust from the ground and laid it on the blind man's eyes. Then He told him to go and wash it off in a pond nearby, which was called the Pool of Siloe. The blind man felt his way slowly down to the pool and washed his eyes, and when he had done it he found that he could see just as well as if he had never been blind at all.

When he got home that night, his neighbors saw him and they said to each other, "Isn't that the man who sat and begged all day because he was blind?"

Some of them answered, "So it is!" But some others said, "No, of course, it can't be. But he is like him!" But the man who had been blind told them, "I am the same man!"

Then, of course, everybody wanted to know what had happened. The man told them, "That Man who is called Jesus made clay and put it on my eyes, and He told me to go and wash in the Pool of Siloe, and I went, and I washed, and now I can see!"

They asked him then where Jesus was now, but he didn't know. Then they decided that the Pharisees ought to hear about it, so they brought the man to them, and he told his story all over again.

It was the Sabbath Day when all this happened, so you can guess what the Pharisees said: "Jesus cannot be a good man, or He would not have done this on the Sabbath!"

But a few of them had better sense, and they said, "If He is a sinner, how is it that He can do such miracles?"

And they all argued about it. Then some of them turned to the man who had been blind and asked, "What have you to say about Him?"

And he answered, "He is a prophet."

The Pharisees continued arguing after that, and presently they thought perhaps this man had never been blind at all, and the whole story was invented. So they sent for his parents and, when they came, asked them about it. His parents were frightened at having to come and speak to the Pharisees, and they would only say that this man was certainly their son, and that he had been born blind, but that how it was he could now see they knew no better than anyone else! And they added that their son was quite old enough to answer for himself! The reason they were so frightened was that they were afraid that if they seemed to be on our Lord's side, the Pharisees might have them put out of the syn-agogue. This was an awful thing to happen to anybody, something like being excommunicated is now — you couldn't go to church, and nobody wanted to have any-thing to do with you.

When the Pharisees found that they could get no help from the man's parents, they sent for the son again, and when he had come they said, "Give glory to God. We know that this Man Jesus is a sinner." They meant this as a hint that the man had better say that he didn't really believe it was our Lord's doing that his eyes were cured. But the man said, "I do not know whether He is a sinner. But I know one thing: I was blind, and now I can see."

The Pharisees said again, "What did He do to you? How did He make you able to see?"

He answered, "I have told you all that before. Do you want to hear it over again? Are you going to become His disciples?" That made the Pharisees very angry, as you can imagine! They began to lose their tempers and to call him names, and they ended up with, "You can be His disciple — we follow Moses. We know that God spoke to Moses, but we do not even know where this Man Jesus comes from!"

The man who had been blind answered, "Why, this is a wonderful thing! You don't even know where He comes from, and He has made me able to see! Now, we know that God does not listen to sinners, but He hears those who do His will. It has never been heard that a man born blind was given his sight, not from the beginning, of the world. Unless this Man were on God's side, He could not do anything."

The Pharisees were furious. They shouted, "Are *you* teaching *us*?"

And they threw him out of the synagogue then and there. Afterward, our Lord found him and said to him, "Do you believe in the Son of God?"

He answered, "Who is He, Lord? Tell me, so that I may believe in Him."

Jesus answered, "You have seen Him. It is He who is talking with you now."

The man who had been blind said, "I believe, Lord." And he fell down before our Lord and adored Him.

Seven

The King's Friends
and His Enemies

After this, our Lord sent seventy-two of His disciples to preach in the cities and towns that He intended to go to later Himself, so that they might prepare the people a little to receive Him. He told the seventy-two to heal the sick and to say everywhere, "The kingdom of God is at hand."

I do not know how long these disciples were away, but when they came back to our Lord they were very pleased and happy indeed, and they said, "The devils also do what we tell them when we speak in Your name!"

Our Lord answered, "I have been watching Satan falling like lightning from Heaven." He had seen the devils they cast out falling as fast as lightning out of the sky! Our Lord went on, "Behold, I have given you power to tread on poisonous snakes without being hurt, as well as power over devils. But do not rejoice because of these things; rejoice because your names are written in Heaven."

A little while after that, while Jesus was teaching, a lawyer, who was a Pharisee, stood up among the people listening and asked a question, "Which is the greatest commandment of all?"

Our Lord answered, "Thou shalt love the Lord thy God with thy whole heart, and with thy whole soul, and with thy whole mind. And the second is this: Thou shalt love thy neighbor as thyself. There is no other commandment greater than these."

The young lawyer answered, "Well, Master, You have said truly that there is one God, and that He should be loved with a man's whole heart, and whole understanding, and whole soul, and whole strength, and that to love one's neighbor is a greater thing than all the offerings a man can make in the Temple."

When He had heard this, our Lord said, "You are not far from the kingdom of God." You see, there were some nice Pharisees, even if most of them were our Lord's enemies. But this one had not quite finished: he wanted to have everything quite clear, so he asked another question, "Who is my neighbor?"

To answer him, our Lord told this story: "A certain man went on a journey from Jerusalem to Jericho, and on the way thieves set upon him and robbed him. They took even his clothes and wounded him, and left him half dead. It happened that a priest was making the same journey, and he saw the wounded man lying there and passed by on the other side of the road. Next came another man, a Jew, who also saw him and passed by. But a foreigner from Samaria who saw him there was sorry for him and bound up his wounds. When he had done that he set him on his own horse and brought him to a hotel, where he stayed the night and looked after him. The next day, when he had to leave, he gave the hotel keeper money to look after him, and said that if he used more it would be all right, because he would repay it on his return journey. Which of these men do you think was a neighbor to the man who was robbed?"

The young lawyer answered, "The merciful one."

And our Lord said, "Go and do as he did."

Presently, on their journeyings, our Lord and His disciples came to a little town called Bethany, which was near Jerusalem. There He went to stay with a man called Lazarus and his two sisters, Martha and Mary.

When they arrived Martha began to be terrifically busy about getting supper and making beds and all the things that people do when guests arrive to stay with them. But Mary came and sat down near our Lord and listened to all He was saying, because she did not want to miss a word.

When Martha saw this, she came to our Lord and said, "Lord, don't You see that my sister is leaving me to do all the work? Tell her to come and help me!"

But our Lord answered, "Martha, Martha, you are worrying about so many things, but only one thing is necessary. Mary has chosen the best thing to do, and no one shall prevent her."

That really was the best thing to do, wasn't it? To listen to our Lord and not bother so much about the supper? But our Lord didn't mean that we ought to go off and say our prayers when our mother or somebody wants us to do something for them!

Perhaps our Lord taught Mary the prayer that He taught His disciples a little while later:

> Our Father,
> who art in Heaven,
> hallowed be Thy name.
>
> Thy Kingdom come.
> Thy will be done,
> on earth as it is in Heaven.
>
> Give us this day
> our daily bread;
> and forgive us
> our trespasses
> as we forgive those
> who trespass against us.
>
> And lead us
> not into temptation,
> but deliver us from evil.
>
> Amen.

You have said that prayer a great many times, haven't you? It is the very best prayer of all, you know, because it is the one our Lord Himself taught to His disciples. After He had taught them that prayer, He warned them that if they did not forgive other people, God would not forgive them. And He taught them something else about prayer.

"Suppose one of you," He said, "had a friend who arrived at your house late one night, after a long journey. If you had no bread, and he was hungry, you would go to one of your neighbors and wake him up by knocking on the door, and shouting to him to give you a loaf. Suppose he called down, 'Don't bother me. It is late, and I am in bed, and the children are asleep.'

"If you really wanted the bread very much you would keep on knocking and calling until he came down and got you the bread because he was so tired of the noise you were making. Well, that is the way to pray: everyone who asks receives, and everyone who seeks finds."

All this time the Pharisees' tempers were getting worse and worse. Some of them saw our Lord cast out a devil, and they said, "He can do that because He is friends with Beelzebub, the prince of the devils."

But our Lord said, "How can Satan cast out Satan? If Satan has risen up against his own devils, his kingdom must be going to fall! But if I cast out devils by the power of God, then the kingdom of God must have come."

The Pharisees had no more to say about that, but they soon thought of something else, for they did not care if what our Lord said was true or not, but only if they could defeat Him. That was what made Him so angry with them.

Here are some of the things He said to them:

> Woe to you scribes and Pharisees,
> hypocrites; because you love the grandest
> seats in the synagogue, and to be bowed
> to where everyone can see it.

> Woe to you scribes and Pharisees,
> hypocrites; because you shut the kingdom
> of Heaven against men: for you yourselves
> do not enter into it, and those who would
> like to go in, you prevent.

Of course, that didn't make them feel any better, and anyone but our Lord would have been afraid of what they might do to Him, for they were determined that He must be stopped from teaching, even if it meant killing Him.

Our Lord knew all about that, of course, and He told His followers, "The disciple is not above his master, nor the servant above his Lord. It is enough for the disciple if he is equal with his master and for the servant if he is equal with his Lord. You see how they treat me, so do not be surprised if they treat you badly: for if they have called the man of the house Beelzebub, what will they call his servants?

"But I say to you, my friends, do not be afraid of people who can kill your bodies and after that have no more that they can do. Fear God, who has power to send you to Hell."

That sounds rather frightening, but our Lord went on: "Are not two sparrows sold for a penny, and not one of them is forgotten by God? God has even counted all the hairs on your heads! Fear not, then; you are worth much more than a great many sparrows! Everyone who is willing to say he believes in me before men, I shall be ready to speak for in Heaven. You will be brought before judges as prisoners because you are my followers, but do not worry about what you are to say, for the Holy Spirit will teach you."

Our Lord was beginning to get them ready for all the things that were to happen to them in only a few months' time, when they would have to go and preach to the whole world after He had ascended into Heaven. It was time now for them to begin to understand about that better, but if they had been told to begin with, perhaps they would have been too frightened to stay with our Lord at all.

He went on now: "Do not worry about your food, nor your clothes. Think of the ravens. They never sow or reap grain or gather it into barns to make bread, and God feeds them. You are much more valuable than ravens! And which of you by thinking hard can grow an inch taller? If you can't even do that, why do you worry so about so many things? Think of the lilies in the fields. They do no work; they don't spin thread to be woven into cloth for clothes. But I say to you that not even King Solomon in all his glory was dressed like one of these. Now, if God clothes the flowers in the fields so well, surely He will look after you, O you of little faith. Do not worry, then, about what you are to eat and drink and wear. Heathen people seek after all these things, but your Father knows you need them. Look first for the kingdom of God and His justice, and these other things that you need will come all right."

Our Lord taught them many more things, too, that you can read in the Gospels.

You know that the Kingdom and the King were promised to the God's Chosen People, the Jews, in the beginning, and it was to them that our Lord preached first of all. If they had all accepted Him, the new worldwide Kingdom would have grown out of the religion God had given His Chosen People, and nowadays there would be no separate Jewish religion and no synagogues, but only Catholics and Catholic churches. It would have made no difference whether people were Jewish or not, except that the ones who were Jewish would have had an extra reason for loving our Lord and His Kingdom. But many of the Jews in our Lord's time did not understand that, and in the end, the Kingdom had to be founded in spite of them, instead of as their own.

The first time our Lord began to explain that this would happen if they were not careful was at a dinner in the house of a Pharisee, where most of the guests were Pharisees, too. One of them said to him, "Blessed is he who shall eat bread in the kingdom of God."

Our Lord turned to him, and told him this parable: "A certain man made a great supper and invited a great many guests. When it was time for the supper to begin he sent his servant to tell the people he had invited that it was time to come. But his guests all began to make excuses. The first one said, 'I have bought a farm, and I have to go and see it. Please excuse me.' And another said, 'I have bought some new oxen, and I must go and try them. Please excuse me.' (Oxen were used for plowing in Palestine then; they still are now.) And still another said, 'I have just gotten married, and so I cannot come.' Every one of the men who had been invited seemed to have an excuse — not one of them would come! When the servant came back to his master and told him all this, his master was angry. He said, 'Go out quickly into the streets and lanes of the city, and bring to the supper the poor and the feeble and the blind and the lame.' The servant came back presently and said, 'Master, I have done as you commanded, and there is still room for more guests.' And his master said, 'Go out again and look for people along the highways and under the hedges, and make them come, so that my house may be filled. But I say to you that none of those who were first invited shall taste my supper.' "

The guests who were invited first were the Jews, and we are all the people who were collected from the roadsides and hedges and ditches to fill their places! I do not know if the Pharisees our Lord was talking to understood that, but I do know that they still kept complaining about everything He did.

This is what He told them once when they complained again that He made friends with publicans and sinners: "If a man had a hundred sheep and one of them strayed from the flock, wouldn't he leave the ninety-nine in the mountains and go looking for the one lost one? And if he found it, wouldn't he be happier about that than about the ninety-nine that had not strayed away? Just so, there shall be joy in Heaven for one sinner doing penance more than for ninety-nine good men who do not need to do penance. Or if a woman has ten pieces of money and loses one, doesn't she sweep the house and look for it with a light until she finds it? And when it is found she will call together all her friends and tell them, 'I have found my money!' So shall there be joy among all the angels of God when one sinner does penance."

I do not know what the Pharisees, who were always so busy explaining how very good they were, thought of that. But our Lord thought it so important to impress on them (and on us) how much God wants sinners to return to Him, that He told one of the most famous of all His stories to explain it better still. Here is the story:

"A certain man had two sons, and the younger one said to his father, 'Instead of making us wait till you die, give us now what you mean us to have then.' His father decided to do that, and he divided all that was to be theirs between his two sons. A few days later the younger son took all his money and traveled away to a far-off country, and there he enjoyed himself spending it. But when it was all spent there began to be a great shortage of food in that country, and presently everybody was hungry, and he was hungry, too. So he went and got work with a farmer, who set him to look after his pigs and feed them. He was so hungry that he would have liked to eat the food he had to give the pigs, and no one would give him a meal.

"After a time he came to himself and thought, 'How many hired men in my father's household have all they want to eat, while I am here starving? I will go home to my father and say to him, 'Father, I have sinned against Heaven and before you. I am not worthy to be called your son any longer, but make me one of your hired men.' And he set out on his journey home.

"While he was still a long way off his father saw him coming, and he was so sorry for his poor, silly son that he ran up the road to meet him, and kissed him. And his son said, as he had planned, 'Father, I have sinned against Heaven and before you, and I am not worthy to be called your son —' But his father would not let him finish. He was calling to his servants to bring good clothes and shoes for his son, and telling them to kill a calf that had been fattened for a great occasion, and he was arranging for a feast, and all kinds of dancing and gaiety. 'Because,' he said, 'my son was dead and is alive

again; he was lost and is found!' So guests were invited to a great dinner and there was music and dancing.

"Now, the elder son was working in the fields while all this was going on, and he knew nothing about it until he came home in the evening and heard the music and the dancing. He wondered what in the world could have happened, so he called one of the servants to him in the garden and asked him why there was a party. 'Your brother has come home safe,' said the servant, 'and your father has made a feast for him, because he is so glad to see him again.'

"When the elder son heard that, he began to sulk and would not go in to the party. But his father heard he had come and went out to ask him why he stayed outside. The elder son said, 'I have always lived at home and done everything you wanted me to, and you have never given me any kind of party for my friends. And now my brother, who wasted all his money, has come home, and you have even killed the special fattened calf for him!'

"His father said, 'Son, you are always with me, and all that I have is yours. But it was right to be merry and glad for your brother was dead and is alive again; he was lost and is found!' "

So God always welcomes us as soon as we are sorry for our sins and begin to go back to Him. But He does not like us to be ungrateful. Our Lord liked people to thank Him, just as we do.

One day He was journeying through Samaria into Galilee and ten men who were lepers came to meet Him. Lepers are people who have leprosy, which is a terrible disease.

Luckily not many people have it now, and in England and America hardly anyone. But in our Lord's time, and for long after, it was very common. It is catching, like measles, only it takes much longer to catch it. The bad thing about it is that, unlike measles, it lasts for years and years and keeps on getting worse until at last the person who has it dies. When anyone got leprosy he had to go away and live by himself, or with other people who had it, too, so that he would not give it to anyone else.

You can see what an awful thing it was to find you had leprosy and must go away from your family and friends, to live by yourself far out in the country, and never to go near anyone again, unless he were a leper, too. And you can see how a man would feel who was cured of leprosy!

Well, these ten lepers met our Lord. They stood at a distance from Him, as they knew they must, and cried out, "Jesus, Master, have mercy on us!"

Our Lord called back to them, "Go and show yourselves to the priests!" The priests in the Jewish religion had charge of deciding who had leprosy and who had not. Now, while these ten lepers were on their way to the priests to show themselves, as our Lord had told them, they suddenly found that the leprosy was all gone, and that they were perfectly well again. One of them, when he saw this, came running back to our Lord, glorifying God as he came, and he fell down at Jesus' feet and thanked Him with all his heart. And this man was a foreigner, a Samaritan.

Our Lord said, "Were not ten cured? And where are the other nine? No one has returned to give glory to

God except this foreigner." And to the Samaritan He said, "Arise, and go your way. Your faith has made you well."

One day the Pharisees asked our Lord when the kingdom of God would come. He told them, "You will not see it coming. People will not be saying, 'Look, it is there!' Or, 'Look, it is here!' For the kingdom of God is already in your midst." And so it was — our Lord, its King, and the Apostles, His first subjects — but of course the Pharisees did not know that.

Even the Apostles didn't really know what kind of kingdom it was going to be, or what kind of king they had. When some mothers brought their children and babies to see our Lord, the Apostles tried to make them go away and not bother Him. But our Lord heard and called to them, "Let the children come to me, for the Kingdom of Heaven is for such as these." And He kissed and blessed them all before their mothers took them home.

Afterward He showed them what kind of people were going to have the hardest time getting into His Kingdom, and they were as surprised as they had been about the children.

A rich young man came running up to Jesus and knelt at His feet. "Good Master," he said, "what must I do to have everlasting life?"

Our Lord answered, "Why do you call me good? Only God is good." (Perhaps He wondered whether the rich young man had guessed who He was!) "You know the commandments."

"Yes," said the rich young man, "and I have kept them all since I was a child." It must have sounded less boastful than it does to us, for our Lord looked at him and loved him. He said, "One thing more is needed for you. Sell all you have, and give the money to the poor. Then come and follow me, and you shall have treasure in Heaven."

But the rich young man was very rich indeed, and he could not bear the idea of doing all that. So he went sadly away. Then our Lord turned to His Apostles and said, "How difficult it is for a rich man to enter the kingdom of Heaven! It is easier for a camel to go through the eye of a needle than for a rich man to enter the kingdom of Heaven."

You can guess how astonished the Apostles were, for they were very like us, and thought it would be lovely to be rich. They began to ask each other, and then our Lord, "Who can be saved then?"

Our Lord answered, "For men by themselves it would be impossible, but to God all things are possible."

Peter said, "We have left all things and followed You: what reward shall we have?"

And our Lord told him and the other Apostles these very exciting things: "You who have followed me shall sit on twelve thrones and judge the twelve tribes of Israel. And everyone who has left house or brothers or sisters or father or mother or wife or children or country for the kingdom of God's sake, shall receive a hundred times as much, now, in this world — houses and brothers and sisters and mothers and children and lands (with persecutions) — and in the world to come, they shall receive life everlasting."

Wasn't it odd that our Lord said "with persecutions," as though they were part of the reward! But you know all that He said then has been coming true again and again ever since, and you can see it happening! The people who leave most for the kingdom of God's sake are priests and monks and nuns, aren't they? And don't they get heaps of brothers and sisters, and mothers who have no children, and children who have no parents, to look after? And don't people give them houses or help them to build houses, and don't they have gardens and grounds, and when they go on the foreign missions, new countries? And they get persecutions, too, just as our Lord said.

So if you ever hear anyone say, "There must be something wrong with the Catholic Church. Look at the beautiful houses these monks and nuns live in! They seem to be rich instead of poor," or, "There is something the matter with these Catholics. They are always in trouble in some country or other," you can remind them that these are just the things that our Lord said would happen to His best friends!

Do you remember Lazarus and Martha and Mary, his sisters, who lived at Bethany, where our Lord once stayed with them?

Well, Lazarus fell ill, and his sisters were afraid he was going to die, so they sent a messenger to our Lord to say, "Lord, he whom You love is sick."

Jesus sent back this mysterious message, "He is not ill enough to die, except for the glory of God, that the Son of God may be glorified by it."

Our Lord was very fond of Lazarus and his sisters, and they must have been disappointed when they got that message and wondered what it meant. Jesus stayed away from them for two whole days after He had sent it, and then He said to His disciples, "Let us now go back again."

The disciples answered, "Last time You were there the people tried to stone You. Surely You had better not go there again."

But He answered, "Lazarus our friend is asleep, and I must go and wake him."

The disciples said, "If he is asleep he must be getting better." They thought our Lord meant he was really asleep, but He meant that he was sleeping in death. You remember He said the same thing about Jairus's little daughter. When He saw that they did not understand He told them plainly, "He is dead. And I am glad for your sakes that I was not there. But now let us go to him."

Thomas said to the others, "Let us go with Him, and if He is killed, we will die, too."

When they arrived at Lazarus's house at Bethany, near Jerusalem, they found that he had been dead for four days and was already buried. In those days people used to be buried in a cave cut out of rock, with a big, flat stone rolled against the door to close it. A great many of Martha's and Mary's friends had come to see them, to comfort them, as people had come to Jairus's home when his daughter died.

As soon as Martha heard that Jesus was coming she went out to meet Him, but Mary sat at home. When Martha had found Jesus she said to Him, "Lord, if You had been here, my brother would not have died. But now I know that whatever You ask of God, God will give You."

Jesus said, "Your brother will rise again."

Martha answered, "I know he will rise again in the resurrection at the last day."

But our Lord did not mean that. He said, "I am the Resurrection and the Life. Whoever believes in me, although he be dead, shall live, and everyone who lives and believes in me, shall never die. Do you believe this?"

Martha answered, "Yes, Lord, I believe that You are the Christ, the Son of the living God, who has come into the world." Then she went back to the house and found Mary and said, "The Master has come, and He is asking where you are." As soon as Mary heard this, she got up and went out to meet our Lord, for He was still on the same part of the road where He had met Martha.

The people who were trying to comfort her thought she was going to Lazarus's grave, and they followed her.

But she went straight to our Lord and knelt down at His feet and said, just as Martha had, "Lord, if you had been here, my brother would not have died."

Our Lord was sad when He saw how miserable she and all the other people were, and He asked, "Where have you laid him?"

Mary answered, "Lord, come and see."

And our Lord wept. Some of the people who saw it said, "Look how He loved Lazarus." But others said, "Couldn't He have kept Lazarus from dying, when He could give sight to a man who was born blind?"

When they had brought our Lord to the grave, He said, "Take away the stone." Martha did not want this done; she said Lazarus had been buried too long, but our Lord reminded her of what He had said: "Did I not tell you that if you believe, you shall see the glory of God?"

Then she let them take the stone away, and Jesus looked up toward Heaven and said, "Father, I give you thanks that You have heard me. I know that You hear me always, but I speak because of the people here, that they may know that You have sent me."

When He had said this He called out aloud, "Lazarus, come forth!" And Lazarus, who had been dead for four days, came walking out of the grave! He was quite well and all right, except that he was still wrapped in the linen clothes he had been buried in. When our

Lord saw this He said to the people about, "Undo those things, and let him go."

Many of the people who had seen this miracle believed in our Lord — isn't it odd that not all of them did? — but some of them went to the Pharisees and told them all about it. Then the Pharisees and chief priests held a council and decided that if things went on like this, everyone would be following Jesus. And from that day on they plotted against Him much harder than before.

In the meantime, Jesus took His disciples away into a lonely part of the country, and they stayed there until the feast of the Passover came around. His enemies waited to see if He would come to Jerusalem for the feast days. They had commanded that anyone who knew where He was should tell them, so that our Lord might be made a prisoner.

Eight

The King Prepares
to Leave the World

A great many people arrived in Jerusalem the day before the feast days began, and they went to the Temple to see if Jesus was there, too. When they found that our Lord had not yet arrived, they said to each other, "He has not come. What do you think that means?"

But Jesus was planning to come.

He called the Apostles to Him and explained to them what was going to happen: "Behold, we are going up to Jerusalem, and all that the prophets foretold about the Son of Man is going to happen there. He will be betrayed to the chief priests and the scribes, and they will hand Him over to the Gentiles, and He will be mocked and scourged and spat upon, and condemned to die. And they will kill Him, and the third day He will rise again from death." *Gentiles* means any people, like us, who are not Jews.

The Apostles heard Him, but they could not understand that such things were really to happen to their Master. They understood so little that John and James went to our Lord with their mother to ask Him a favor.

When our Lord saw them coming He said, "What do you want?"

Their mother answered, "Say that my two sons may sit, one on Your right and the other on Your left, in Your Kingdom." She meant that she wanted Him to give them the two best and grandest jobs in His government.

Our Lord turned to James and John and said, "You do not know what you are asking! Can you drink the cup that I shall drink?" He meant, "Can you suffer and die as I am going to?"

They certainly did not know what they were asking for, but they said, "We can."

Our Lord answered, "You shall indeed drink my chalice, but I cannot promise that you shall sit on my right hand or my left: my Father has arranged who shall sit there."

When the other ten Apostles heard what James and John had done they were angry, and I'm not surprised. But our Lord called them and said, "You know that the kings of the Gentiles lord it over them, but it shall not be that way among you. Whoever of you is the greatest shall be like the younger, and whoever is first among you shall be the servant of all the rest, just as I am not here to be worked for, but to work for you." Did you know that the Pope's special title is "Servant of the servants of God"? And this is why — because he is the first and greatest among us.

On the way to Jerusalem our Lord and the Apostles and disciples came to Jericho, and near the city Jesus cured two blind men. These two followed them into the town, and a great crowd gathered and went with them as well.

In Jericho there lived a rich tax-collector named Zaccheus who very much wanted to see Jesus, but he was a little man, too short to see over the heads of the people in the crowd. So, like a small boy, he climbed up a sycamore tree that grew by the roadside.

I don't suppose he expected anyone to see him up there, but our Lord looked straight up into the tree and said to him, "Make haste and come down, Zaccheus, I want to visit your house today."

Zaccheus was delighted that our Lord was coming to his house, and he climbed quickly down the tree and brought our Lord and the Apostles to his home.

Some of the people in the crowd said, "He is going to be a guest in the house of a man who is a sinner."

But Zaccheus, standing in front of our Lord in his house, said, "Behold, Lord, I am going to give half of everything I have to the poor, and to every man

I have wronged, I will give four times as much as I took from him."

Jesus said, "Salvation has come to your house today." After our Lord left Zaccheus He went on to Bethany again, where Lazarus lived, which I expect you remember was near Jerusalem.

There they made a great supper for Him and His Apostles. Lazarus sat at table with our Lord, and Martha served the supper. But Mary brought a box of very precious, sweet-smelling ointment, and she broke it open and rubbed our Lord's feet with it.

I expect His feet were sore and tired with walking all day, and that it made them feel much more comfortable to have them rubbed with ointment. Everyone in the house could smell the sweet scent of it, and they could tell that it was very expensive.

Judas said, "What is the use of such waste? This ointment might have been sold for a great deal of money, and the money could have been given to the poor." Judas said this, not because he cared about the poor, but because he liked money. He carried the purse with the money for our Lord and all the Apostles, and he thought that he might very well have been one of the poor people to whom the money was given!

But our Lord took Mary's part again, saying, "Let her alone. The poor you always have with you, and you can be kind to them whenever you like. But you will not always have me. And I say to you, wherever this gospel is preached in the whole world, what she has done will be told in memory of her."

The King Prepares to Leave the World

The next day, our Lord set out on the last part of His journey to Jerusalem, and on the way He came to Mount Olivet, on which Bethany is built and which is very near to the city.

There He sat down to rest, but He called two of His disciples and said to them, "Go into the nearest village, and there you will find an ass and her colt. Loose them, and bring them to me. If anyone asks you what you are doing, tell them that the Master has need of them, and he will let you take them at once."

The two disciples did just as He told them, and the man who owned the ass and her colt let them go, just as Jesus had said he would. When they had brought them to Him the disciples laid some of their clothes on the colt, instead of a saddle, and our Lord rode toward Jerusalem on him. Meantime, the people in the city had heard that He had been seen at Bethany, so they came out to meet Him.

When the people saw Him coming, riding on the colt, they laid branches of palms on the road before Him, and threw down their clothes for Him to ride over, and they shouted and sang, "Hosanna to the Son of David! Blessed is He who comes in the name of the Lord! Blessed be the kingdom of our father David that comes! Peace in Heaven and glory on high!" *Hosanna* is a sort of cheer something like "Hooray!"

There were even some of the Pharisees among those who had come to meet Him, and when they heard what the crowds were singing they said, "Master, make them stop singing that!"

But Jesus answered, "If they are silent, the stones will cry out!"

When they came to a part of the road from which they could see Jerusalem, our Lord wept, and He said, "If you had only known in time the things that are for your happiness! But now they are hidden from your eyes. For the time shall come when your enemies will dig a trench about you, and come upon you from every side. They will not leave a single stone of your buildings upon another stone." And what He had said came true thirty-seven years later, when the Romans destroyed the whole city and all the buildings were knocked down.

When they came to Jerusalem, the whole city heard the noise of singing, and they said to each other, "Who is this?" And everyone in the procession answered, "Jesus the Prophet, from Nazareth in Galilee."

Our Lord went to the Temple, and there for almost the last time the lame and sick and blind were brought to Him, and He cured them all. And there were children in the Temple singing and crying out, "Hosanna to the Son of David!"

The chief priests and the scribes, who, I am sure, were the sort of people who don't much like children anyway, were angry, and they said to Jesus, "Do you hear what these children are saying?"

And He answered, "Yes. Have you never read in the Scriptures where it says, 'Out of the mouths of children and babies you have brought perfect praise'?"

In the evening He went back to Bethany for the night. If He had stayed in Jerusalem the chief priests and the scribes and Pharisees surely would have thought of an excuse to arrest Him and put Him in prison while it was quiet and His friends and the crowds who followed Him were all asleep.

He did not go to Martha's house, for fear of getting His friends into trouble, I suppose. Instead He rested among the olive trees in a garden called Gethsemane. The next day He came back to the Temple and taught there, and then went back to Bethany again for the night.

The day after that, when He was in the Temple, the chief priests and the scribes came to Him and said, "By what authority are you doing these things, and who gave you this authority?"

Jesus answered, "I also will ask you a question; and if you tell me the answer, then I also will tell you by what authority I do these things. Was John's baptism from Heaven, or was it from men?" He meant, "Did John baptize because God wanted him to, or was it just an idea of his own?"

The men who had come to question Him did not know what to say, for they thought, "If we say, 'From Heaven,' He will answer, 'Then why did you not believe him?' but if we say, 'From men,' everybody in Jerusalem will turn upon us and stone us to death, for they were all sure that John was a prophet." So they said, "We do not know."

And our Lord answered, "Then neither will I tell you by what authority I do these things. But what do you think of this? There was a man who had two sons, and one day he said to the eldest, 'Son, go and work in my vineyard,' and the son answered, 'I will not.' But presently he was sorry, and went after all. The father went to his younger son and said the same thing, and the second son answered, 'I will go,' but then he did not. Which of the two did what their father wanted?"

They could only answer, "The first."

Jesus said, "I say to you that the publicans and sinners will go into the kingdom of God before you. For John came to you, and you did not believe him, but they believed in John.'"

It was not much use for the Pharisees and their friends to say how good they were, and how bad the publicans and sinners were, was it? It was the publicans and sinners who had done what John told them and the "good" people who had taken no notice of what he said.

We have now come almost to the end of our Lord's time of preaching. All these last days before He was arrested are full of His warnings to His nation of what would happen to them if they did what they were determined to do — put Him to death.

Here is another story He told them to explain, if possible, what was happening: "A certain man planted a vineyard, and because he had to go on a long journey and stay in a country far away, he rented it to other men, who were to pay their rent in grapes from his vines. When it was harvest time he sent one of his servants for the fruit, but the men in charge of the vineyard beat him and sent him away without any. So he sent another servant, and they beat him, too, and wounded his head and sent him back with nothing. He sent a third, and they killed him. Then he sent several more, one after the other, and all of them were killed or stoned or beaten. Last of all he thought, 'I will send my only son, for surely they will have some respect for him.' So he sent his son. But when the men in the vineyard saw him, and knew who he was, they said to each other, 'This is the owner's heir, who will have the vineyard when his father dies. If we kill him, we can keep it forever.' So they took him out of the vineyard and killed him. Now, when the master of the vineyard comes home, what do you think he will do to them?"

The men listening cried out, "He will bring those evil men to an evil end, and he will give the vineyard to others, who will send him the fruit when they should."

And our Lord answered, "Therefore I say to you that the kingdom of God will be taken away from you and given to a nation who will give God its fruit."

He meant (and they understood it when they had had time to think) that God had chosen the Jews out of the whole world to be the nation to which He would come, and in which He would found his Kingdom, and He had sent them prophets again and again to tell them what they should do in return, and all of them had been treated badly, and many of them killed. And now God had sent His Son, and they meant to kill Him, too.

If they did, what could they expect? But although the meaning was so plain, and although they ought to have known that our Lord had authority from God by the wonderful things He did, they still would not believe Him, and only wanted to kill Him all the more.

But they dared not arrest Him openly, especially just then, for the city was full of Galileans, the people who knew our Lord best, and who had come to Jerusalem for the feast days. His enemies knew they must either turn the people against Him, or trick Him into saying something that would make the Romans angry.

And this is one of the plans they thought of. They sent some of their followers to Him, pretending to want an answer to a difficult question. They said, "We know that You always say just what You think. Now tell us, is it lawful to pay taxes to Caesar or not?" Caesar was the head of the Roman empire, as I am sure you know, and they asked our Lord this, because if He said yes all the people in the country who hated paying taxes to a foreign nation would be angry with Him, and if He said no they could tell the Romans, who would arrest Him for speaking against their government.

But Jesus did not say either yes or no. He said, "You hypocrites! Why do you ask me such a thing? Show me the coin you have to pay." They showed it to Him, and it had a picture of a head with some writing on it, as many coins have today. Our Lord said, "Whose portrait is this, and whose name is written on it?"

They could only answer, "Caesar's," for so it was. Our Lord said, "Give therefore to Caesar the things that belong to Caesar, and to God the things that belong to God."

There was no answer to that, was there, and no need for Caesar or anyone else to be angry?

After this our Lord was questioned again, this time by the Sadducees, a tiresome sort of people, who did not believe in the resurrection of our bodies from the dead, or in a great part of the Holy Scriptures either. And He silenced them too. But when He saw how every sort of leader and wise man in Jerusalem was against Him and determined on His death, He wept over the city, and this is what He said:

> Jerusalem, Jerusalem,
> thou that killest the prophets,

and stonest them
that are sent to thee,
how often would I have
gathered thy children together,
as the hen gathers her chicks
under her wings,
and thou wouldst not!

Behold, your house shall be
left to you, desolate.

For I say to you
that you shall not
see me again until you say:
"Blessed is He who cometh
in the name of the Lord."

And He warned His disciples again that as He had been hated, so would they be. And so they were, and so His followers are, even today.

The kingdom of God is never quite at peace with the world. Just when everything seems safe and quiet, the old troubles start again, and there are new martyrs and new heroes shooting up to Heaven in crowds. So we have always to be ready for trouble: this is never a safe, solid sort of world for Catholics!

Indeed, if you want adventures, a Catholic is the thing to be. If everything is too peaceful for you in your own country you can go as a priest or a sister to the foreign missions, which is one of the most exciting things left to do in the whole world.

Our Lord told His disciples about this time what the signs of the end of the world would be, wars and all kinds of trouble, and He told them that no one could be sure how near or how far away it was, and not to be sad when it seemed to be coming, although everybody else would be, and that they should always be ready, either for death or the end of the world. And they were always to pray, whatever happened. He told them a little of what the end of the world would be like:

> The Son of Man
> shall come in majesty,
> and all the angels with Him,
> and all the nations of the earth
> shall be gathered together before Him,
> and He will separate them
> one from another,
> the wicked from the good,
> as a shepherd separates the sheep
> from the goats in his flock:
>
> And He shall set
> the sheep on His right hand
> and the goats on His left.
>
> Then shall He say to the good
> on His right hand:
>
>> Come, you blessed of my Father,
>> possess the Kingdom prepared
>> for you from the
>> beginning of the world.
>>
>> For I was hungry,
>> and you gave me
>> food to eat;

The King Prepares to Leave the World

I was thirsty,
and you gave me
water to drink;

I was a stranger,
and you made me
your guest;

I had no clothes,
and you gave me some;

I was sick,
and you visited me;

I was in prison,
and you came to see me.

And the good will answer:

Lord, when did
we see You hungry
and feed You;
or thirsty
and give You a drink?

And when did
we see You a stranger
and take You
into our houses?

Or without clothes
and gave You some?

Or when did
we see You sick or in prison
and come to You?

A Life of Our Lord for Children

And the King answering
shall say to them:

As long as you did one of
those things for one of
the least important
of my followers, you did it for me.

Then He will turn
to the people on
His left hand, and
He will say to them:

Depart, you cursed,
into everlasting fire
which was prepared for
the Devil and his angels.

For I was hungry,
and you gave me
no food to eat;

I was thirsty,
and you gave me
no water to drink;

I was a stranger,
and you would not
let me stay in your house;

I had no clothes,
and you would not
give me any;

I was sick and in prison,
and you would not visit me.

The King Prepares to Leave the World

And they also shall say:

> Lord, when did we ever
> see You hungry or thirsty?
>
> Or a stranger,
> or without clothes?
>
> Or sick? Or a prisoner?

And He will answer:

> As long as you did not
> do one of these things
> for the very least important
> of my followers, it is the same
> as if you did not do it for me.

> And those people shall
> go into everlasting punishment,
> but the good shall
> go into life everlasting.

So we had better do things for people who are hungry or sick or in any kind of need, hadn't we? It would be an awful thing to find ourselves on the wrong side of our Lord at the end of the world.

Every day, for these last days of His life, our Lord taught in the Temple, and every night He went into the country, to the Garden of Gethsemane on the Mount of Olives, which is also called Mount Olivet.

Now comes one of the saddest things that ever happened. Judas, one of the twelve Apostles, went to the chief priests and said, "What will you give me if I betray Jesus to you?"

You see, they couldn't arrest our Lord in the daytime, without getting into trouble with the people who wanted Him to be king, and who were sure He was a prophet. But if they found out where He went each evening, and arrested Him by night and thought of a good reason to give, that would be another matter.

Our Lord's enemies promised Judas thirty pieces of silver money — not very much — if he would betray Jesus to them. It seemed enough to him, and he said he would do it as soon as a good chance came.

Now it was the time when the Jews held the Passover feast, which was sometimes called the Pasch. It went on for seven days, as you read in the first part of this story, and the next day was the day when they ate the roasted lamb and wild lettuce. All this week they ate only unleavened bread to remind them of the hurried start their forefathers had made when Moses brought them out of Egypt. The Jews still do this, because they don't know that the lamb was a kind of foretelling of our Lord's death for sinners and that now we have the Holy Mass instead.

The Apostles asked our Lord where they were to arrange to eat this special meal. He told two of them to go into Jerusalem and follow a man they would see carrying a jug of water. They were to go into the house that he entered and tell the man who lived there that the Master wanted to know where the dining room was, where He was to eat the Pasch.

The two Apostles did as they were told, and the man of the house showed them a large dining room, which was all ready for them, and there they prepared the meal.

In the evening Jesus came to the room and sat down at the table with them, and He said, "I have been longing to eat this Pasch with you. For from now on I will not eat it again until it is fulfilled in the kingdom of God." After He had said that, He took a chalice of wine and said, "Take this, and divide it among you. For I will not drink again of this fruit of the vine, until I drink it new with you in the kingdom of God."

Even now, the Apostles began arguing again, about which of them should be the greatest.

But our Lord said, "Which is greater? The man who sits at the table or the one who serves? Isn't it the one who sits at the table? But I am here as the one who serves. You are the twelve who have been with me through all my trials, and I give you, as my Father has given me, a Kingdom."

Then He got up and took a towel and tied it around Him like an apron, and He put water into a basin and came to the Apostles in turn, to wash their feet and dry them on the towel.

He came first to Peter, and Peter was horrified that his Master should be doing such a thing for him. He said, "Lord, are You going to wash my feet!"

Our Lord answered, "You do not understand now what I am doing, but you will understand presently."

Peter said, "Lord, You shall never wash my feet!"

But our Lord answered, "If I do not wash you, you shall not be my follower."

Poor Peter was distressed at that, and he said "Lord, wash not only my feet, but my hands and my head, too!"

Jesus must have smiled at that, but He only said, "A clean man who washes every day needs only to have his feet washed, and he is quite clean all over."

After that He washed their feet in turn, and then He took off the towel and came and sat down with them again, and He said, "Do you understand what I have done? You call me Master and Lord, and you do well, for so I am. But if I who am your Master and Lord have washed your feet, you ought to wash one another's. The servant is not greater than his Lord nor the apostle greater than the one who sends him."

I don't think they argued anymore after that about which of them was to be the greatest and grandest in the kingdom of God, do you?

Our Lord went on, "He who receives you receives me, and he who receives me receives Him who sent me."

As they were going on with their supper, our Lord spoke again, very sad words: "One of you is going to betray me."

The twelve looked at each other, wondering who it could be, and they were very worried and unhappy.

Now, John was our Lord's special friend among the twelve, and he was sitting next to Him. Peter made a sign to John to ask our Lord who it was. John saw, and he said quietly to Jesus, "Who is it?"

Our Lord answered, "It is the man to whom I shall give a piece of bread dipped." And He dipped a bit of bread in the gravy from the roast lamb they were eating and gave it to Judas. After Judas had eaten it, he got up to go out. Our Lord called to him as he went, "What you are going to do, do quickly."

But none of them understood that Judas was going then to betray Him, not even John. They thought our Lord had told him to go and buy something for the next day, because he was the one who had charge of the money for them all. So Judas went out without anyone trying to stop him, and it was dark.

After he had gone, our Lord did the tremendous thing for which He had begun to prepare His Apostles when He fed five thousand men with a few loaves and fishes, and by His teaching afterward when He said, "I am the bread that came down from Heaven."

He took bread into His hands and broke it and said, "Take and eat. This is my Body." Then He took up the chalice, gave thanks to God, and said, "Take and drink you all of this, for this is my Blood of the New Testament which shall be shed for you, and for many unto the remission of sins. Do this for a commemoration of me."

And so the Apostles received the very first Holy Communion that anyone received, but although it was the first and given by our Lord Himself, you and I receive Him just as truly any day we choose.

Afterward our Lord gave them a new commandment. He said they were to love one another as He had loved them, and He told them that people would know they were His followers by the way they kept this commandment. Then He said, "You will all be shocked at what happens to me tonight, but after I have risen again, I will go before you into Galilee."

Afterward He turned to Peter and spoke to him, calling him by his old name, Simon. He said, "Simon, Simon, Satan hath desired to have you that he may sift you as harvesters sift the grain from the straw when they harvest wheat. But I have prayed for you that your faith should not fail, and once you are converted, you will strengthen your brothers."

St. Peter, you know, was the first Pope, and that prayer was for all the Popes since as well. Some of them have done very odd and sometimes very wrong things, but none of them have failed to teach the true Faith, because our Lord will not let them lead His Church astray.

Peter did not quite understand what that was all about, but he said, "Although everyone else may be shocked and frightened at what happens to You, I will not be. I am ready to go with You into prison, and to death."

Jesus answered, "This very night, before the cock crows, you will deny three times over that you know me."

Peter said all the more certainly, "Although I should die with You, I will not deny that I know You."

And all the other Apostles said the same.

Then our Lord began to tell them more plainly that His life on earth was coming to an end. He comforted them and promised that it was better that He should go back to His Father in Heaven, best even for them, because after He had gone He would send the Holy Spirit to comfort and strengthen them. And He said, "The Holy Spirit, whom the Father will send in my name, will teach you all things and bring to your minds all that I have told you. Peace I leave with you. My peace I give to you. Not as the world gives, give I unto you."

Then they got up from the table and set out on the way to the Garden of Gethsemane.

Our Lord was taking them to rest under the olive trees again, and on the way He went on teaching them.

He told them many things they had not heard before because this was the last time He was to walk and talk with them before He died.

These are some of the things He told them: "I am the vine, and you are the branches. If branches are cut off from a vine, they are useless; branches are no good by themselves, and neither are you — you cannot do anything alone. Without me you can do nothing, but if you live in me, you will bear much fruit. And you shall ask whatever you will, and it shall be done for you. This is my commandment: that you love one another as much as I have loved you. No man can love more than this, that he will lay down his life for his friends. You are my friends, if you do the things I command you. I will not call you servants, for a servant does not know his master's plans, but I call you friends, because all the things I have heard from my Father I have told you.

"If the world hates you, remember that it hated me first. Remember what I told you — the servant is not greater than the master. If they have persecuted me, they will also persecute you, if they have done as I told them, they will do as you tell them, too. The time is coming when whoever kills one of you will think that he is doing a service for God. But I have told you these things beforehand, so that when they begin to happen you can remember that I told you what to expect. You are sad now, but I will see you again, and your hearts will rejoice, and your joy will never be taken away from you! In the world you will have distress, but have confidence; I have overcome the world."

Our Lord prayed, too, for the Apostles and for all who, through their teaching would come to believe in Him — and that includes us.

When Jesus and the Apostles reached Gethsemane, He said to them, "Sit here, while I go over there and pray." He took Peter and James and John with Him, and He began to be very sorrowful and afraid, and He said to them, "My soul is sorrowful even unto death. Stay here and watch with me."

He went a little way from them then, and fell down on His face and prayed, saying, "Father, if You will, take this chalice away from me. Nevertheless, Your will be done."

Have you ever thought when something that frightened and hurt you was over, "If I had known that was going to happen beforehand how miserable I would have been"?

Well, our Lord knew just exactly what was going to happen to Him, and how terrible it would be. He knew what the nails through His hands would feel like, and how the thorns running into His head would hurt.

But worse than that, He could see all the sins of the world, Adam and Eve's sin, our sins, and all the others there ever have been or will be until the last day. And He was taking them all on His own shoulders so that His death should make up for them all. No wonder He asked His Father whether He really must. If you remember as you read the rest of this book that all our Lord's sufferings were brought about by sin, you will begin to see how terrible a thing sin must be.

God the Father sent an angel to strengthen His Son, and our Lord went on praying.

He was so distressed at the weight and the horror of the sins He was going to die to take away, that His sweat became drops of blood running down to the ground. When He stood up at last and came back to the three Apostles, He found them asleep, and He said to Peter, "Could you not stay awake with me for one hour? Watch and pray, or you may be tempted."

But then He made an excuse for them, "Your souls are willing, but your bodies are weak." They had not meant to go to sleep, but they were very tired, and had not managed to keep their eyes open.

Our Lord went away again and prayed as He had before, and when He came back they were asleep again, and they did not know what to say to Him when they woke.

A third time He went away and prayed, saying the same words again, and when He returned that time He said, "Are you asleep now, and taking your rest? Behold, the time has come, and the Son of Man is going to be betrayed into the hands of sinners. Rise and let us go. Behold, he is here — the man who is going to betray me."

While He was still speaking, they saw Judas coming, and with him a great crowd of people, sent by the chief priests and the Pharisees to arrest Jesus.

They carried swords and clubs and lanterns and torches, and there were enough of them to arrest a hundred men. Judas had given them a sign by which they were to know which of the men in the garden was our Lord. He had told them that he would kiss our Lord, which was how a good disciple greeted his master then, and so they would know who Jesus was. So as soon as he saw Jesus, Judas went up to Him and kissed Him and said, "Hail, Master!"

Our Lord answered, "Friend, what have you come to do?" Then he turned to the crowd and said, "Whom are you looking for?"

They answered, "Jesus of Nazareth," and our Lord said, "I am He."

But they were so frightened, by His look or perhaps by what they had heard of His miracles, that the ones in front went crowding back on the people behind them, and they fell down on the ground. When they

had recovered He asked them again, "Whom are you looking for?"

And again they answered "Jesus of Nazareth," and our Lord said, "I have told you that I am He. If you are looking for me, let the men with me go away."

Then Peter, who had a sword, drew it and struck the servant of the high priest and cut off his ear. But our Lord told him to put his sword away, and He healed the servant's ear, and said to Peter, "Shall I not drink the chalice my Father has given me? Don't you know that if I asked Him, He would give me immediately more than twelve legions of angels?" And to the crowd who had come to arrest Him He said, "You have come out armed with swords and clubs, as though I were a robber. I sat daily teaching in the Temple, and you did not arrest me. But this is your hour and the hour of the power of darkness."

Then the Apostles, all leaving Him, ran away.

Nine

The King Suffers and Dies

The soldiers and all the company who had come to arrest our Lord led Him to the high priest. With them were all His enemies, the other chief priests, the scribes, and all those rich and angry men whom He had treated, not as they were used to being treated, but as they deserved.

Of all the twelve Apostles only Peter dared come back, and he was not brave enough to join our Lord, but he followed behind the crowd that had arrested Him. When they came to the chief priest's house, and went in, Peter slipped into the great hall, too.

There was a big fire there, because it was a cold night, and Peter stood beside it, warming himself. One of the maids who worked for the high priest stared at him, but he did not notice her, until she said, "You were with Jesus of Nazareth." Peter got a terrible shock then, and he answered quickly, "Woman, I do not know Him at all," and he got up and went to the door of the hall, but there another maidservant saw him, and she also said, "Why, this man used to be with Jesus of Nazareth!"

Peter said, "I have never met Him," and about an hour later, while he still stood waiting to see what would be done to our Lord, one of the men standing near him said, "I am sure you are one of Jesus of Nazareth's followers, for you speak like a Galilean." Peter was so frightened that he began to curse and to swear that he did not know our Lord, and as he was still speaking a cock crowed, and Jesus turned and looked at Peter. Then Peter remembered how our Lord had told him that before the cock crowed he would deny Him three times, and he went out of the hall and wept very bitterly. He really was much the bravest of all the Apostles, wasn't he? But still he was not quite so brave as he had expected to be.

While all this was happening, the high priest had been questioning Jesus at the other end of the hall. He asked our Lord about His disciples, and about what He taught. Our Lord answered, "I have always spoken openly, in the synagogues and in the Temple, where anyone could hear. I did not speak secretly. Why do you not ask those who have heard me teach instead of asking me?"

When He had said this one of the servants standing by hit Him and said, "What do You mean by answering the high priest like that?"

Jesus replied, "If I have spoken evil, tell me what it was, but if I have told the truth, why do you strike me?"

Then all the soldiers and servants who were in the hall began to mock Him and to strike Him on His face. And they blindfolded Jesus, who had made so many blind men able to see, and hit Him and said, "Prophesy to us who hit You!"

Next day, early in the morning, the chief priests and the scribes met together to decide what to do with our

Lord next, for they were determined that He should be put to death, but they were not sure what would be the best way to manage it.

They tried calling in witnesses to speak against Him, but as the witnesses could say nothing against Him unless they told lies, they all contradicted each other, and it was hopeless. At last the high priest stood up and spoke to Jesus, saying, "Have You nothing to say? Do You not hear what all these witnesses say about You?" But our Lord answered nothing at all. Then the high priest suddenly came to the point. He said, "Are you the Christ, the Son of the living God?"

Our Lord answered, "I am. And you shall see the Son of Man sitting on the right hand of the power of God, and coming in the clouds of Heaven."

Then the high priest cried out, "Now we have heard Him blaspheme! What do we want with witnesses? What do you think of it?"

And they all answered that our Lord ought to be killed, because He had claimed to be really the Son of God, which, as they understood very well, was the same thing as claiming to be God. Because if you are somebody's son or daughter, you must be the same kind of being they are, mustn't you? Men's sons are men, and God's Son is God.

When Judas saw what he had done to our Lord, he brought the thirty pieces of silver back to the priests, and said, "I have sinned in betraying an innocent man."

But the priests said, "What has that to do with us? It is entirely your affair."

Then Judas threw the money they had given him on the floor of the Temple, and he went and hanged himself.

The priests did not know what to do with the money, because money paid for such a thing was not allowed to be put into the Temple treasury (although they didn't mind paying it, or taking it back). At last they decided to buy a field with it and use it as a burying place for foreigners who happened to die in Jerusalem, and that was what they did.

Our Lord's enemies thought they now had a good excuse for putting our Lord to death, but the Romans would not let them punish anyone by killing him, unless they had judged him, too, and decided that he ought to die. So our Lord was taken next to the Roman governor of Judea, who was called Pilate, and they began to accuse Jesus of all kinds of things.

They said, "We have caught this Man leading people astray. He is telling them to refuse to pay taxes to you, and He says He is Christ the King." Of course that was not the reason they wanted our Lord to die; but they thought it would be very hard to explain to a pagan Roman that a man ought to be killed because he said he was God, so they tried saying all these other things first.

Pilate asked them, "Let me see, just what is it you accuse Him of?"

They answered, "If He was not a criminal, we would not have brought Him to you." Because really they did not know what to accuse Him of!

Pilate answered, "Well, take Him away now, and judge Him according to your own law." But they said, "You do not allow us to put a man to death."

When Pilate understood that they wanted our Lord killed he went back into the room where Jesus was and said to Him, "Are you the King of the Jews?"

Our Lord answered, "Do you say that for yourself, or have others told it to you about me?"

Pilate said, "Am I a Jew? Your own people have brought You to me to be judged. What have You done?"

Jesus answered, "My Kingdom is not of this world. If my Kingdom were of this world, my people would certainly fight to prevent me from being delivered to the Jewish rulers: but my Kingdom is not of the world."

Pilate said, "Are You a King then?"

And our Lord said, "You say that I am a King. For this I was born, and for this I came into the world, that I should be a witness to the truth. Everyone who belongs to the truth listens to me."

Pilate was getting impatient. There seemed to be no reason to be afraid of this kind of king, who said His followers would not fight for Him, and who talked about truth. So Pilate said, "What is truth?" And then he went back to the crowd outside without waiting for an answer. To them he said, "I find no reason to condemn this Man."

But our Lord's enemies called out that He had been telling the people to rebel against Roman rule, all through Judea and in Galilee. Pilate caught one word, "Galilee," and he asked if Jesus came from there. When he had heard that our Lord was from that part of the country, he was very thankful and thought that all this bother was at an end, because he was not governor of Galilee, and that meant that the right man to judge our Lord was King Herod, of all people!

Now, Herod was in Jerusalem for the feast days, so Pilate sent Jesus and His accusers over to the house where he was. Herod, as you know, was very much interested in our Lord, and frightened of Him, for he thought He might be John the Baptist risen from the dead. So he was delighted to hear that He had been taken prisoner, and was to be brought to him to be judged. Herod thought there could be no real danger from a man who could be arrested so easily, but that he might get Jesus to work a miracle for him — something he had wanted to see done for a long time.

When our Lord was brought before him he began to ask all sorts of questions, but our Lord did not answer him at all. When they saw that He would not speak, much less work a miracle, Herod and all his soldiers mocked Him. They dressed Him in a white garment after they had finished and sent Him back to Pilate again. It was usual to dress madmen in white garments, and this was what Herod meant. But it was also usual for men who were about to be made king to wear white, and this Herod forgot. Herod was so pleased that Pilate had thought of sending Jesus to be judged by him that he went and made friends with him that day, although before they had always quarreled.

Pilate still told our Lord's enemies that he could see no reason for punishing Him, and that evidently Herod had not either, since he had simply sent Him back again. When Pilate saw that in spite of this the Jews were still determined that our Lord should be killed, he thought, "I will have Him scourged, and that will content these people who are so furious, and then the Prisoner can go free."

This was all the more convenient because he had to set one prisoner free on that feast day, in any case, and he had another one, called Barabbas, who was a robber and a very unpleasant person indeed. Pilate thought that if he offered them their choice between Jesus and Barabbas, they would be sure to ask for Jesus.

So he went out on the balcony of his house and called to the crowd who were standing in the street below, "Shall I release Barabbas or Jesus?"

If the people in the crowd had been left to themselves, surely they would have chosen our Lord, but the chief priests and Pharisees went about among them and persuaded them to ask for Barabbas.

When they shouted that they wanted Barabbas, Pilate said, "Then what shall I do with your King?"

And the crowd cried out, "Crucify Him!"

Crucifying people, as you know from your own crucifix, is fixing them to a cross and leaving them there to die. It was a horrible way of killing people, but the Romans used it for everyone who was condemned to death. Generally they tied people to the cross with ropes, which was bad enough. They did not usually nail them — not, I am afraid, from kindness, but because it was more trouble.

Pilate still could not understand what all this was about, or why our Lord's own people would want Him killed, so he said, "Why, what evil has He done?"

But the only answer was more shouts of "Crucify Him!"

So Pilate had our Lord scourged. Nothing could have been more unfair, for he knew, and had said, that our Lord had done no wrong.

Scourging was being whipped so hard and so long that the man it was done to often died while it was going on. Our Lord did not die, but wouldn't you think that after that, everyone would have been sorry for Him, even the soldiers themselves?

But they were not. They thought it was a good time for a joke; so they dressed Him in a scarlet cloak of the sort Caesar would wear, and put a reed in His hand and a crown of thorns on His head, and they bowed before Him and said, "Hail, King of the Jews!" And they spat on Him and took away the reed and struck Him on the head with it.

Meantime Pilate was sitting in his judgment seat, waiting for all this to be finished, and while he waited a message came to him from his wife: "Have nothing to do with this good Man, for I have suffered many things in a dream because of Him." I wish we knew what happened to Pilate's wife afterward and if she ever became a Christian.

Pilate sent for water, and he went out onto the balcony and washed his hands where everyone could see him and said, "I am innocent of the blood of this good Man; look to it yourselves."

And all the people answered, "His blood be upon us and upon our children."

Pilate thought he would try still once more. So he brought our Lord out onto the balcony in the scarlet cloak and with the crown of thorns still on His head, and he said, "Behold the Man!"

When the crowd saw Jesus, they cried out, not in pity as you would think, but in rage: "Crucify Him! Crucify Him!"

Pilate said, "You can take Him and crucify Him, but I see no reason why He should be killed."

The chief priests cried out, "We have a law, and that law says that He ought to die, because He said He was the Son of God."

When Pilate heard that, he was frightened. He took Jesus back from the window and said to Him, "Where do You come from?"

But our Lord said nothing. Then Pilate asked, "Won't You even speak to me? Don't You know that I have power to crucify You, or to release You?"

Jesus answered, "You would not have any power at all unless it were given you by God. Therefore the man who handed me over to you is a greater sinner than you are."

From that time on, Pilate kept trying to release our Lord, but it was no use.

When he told the Jews what he intended to do, they shouted, "If you release this Man, you are not Caesar's friend, for whoever makes himself a king is speaking against Caesar."

That was a good idea of theirs, wasn't it? If Pilate released our Lord, they would send word to Caesar that a Man who said He was King of the Jews had been handed over to Pilate for trying to start a revolution and that Pilate had released Him, and what would Caesar think then? Especially as Pilate was a very bad governor and there had been trouble about the way he did things already.

Now Pilate was frightened, but he did not know whether to be more afraid of our Lord and who He might be, or of Caesar and what he might do. So he brought our Lord out onto the balcony again and sat down in his judgment seat and said to the Jews, "Behold your King!"

They shouted again, "Crucify Him! Crucify Him! Let Him be crucified!"

Pilate said, "Do you want me to crucify your King?" But the chief priests answered, "We have no king except Caesar."

And that is how it is that the Kingdom is ours and our Lord's own people do not belong to it. It is a very sad thing, isn't it, that the Jews who had been prepared so long and so carefully by God should not know their great King when He came and should reject Him and say they would rather have a king who was great in this world?

Of course, lots of them have joined the Kingdom since, but it spoiled the plan of making the kingdom of our Lord grow up out of the kingdom of the Jews.

After the Jews had said, "We have no king but Caesar," Pilate could think of nothing else to do, and he had not the courage to do what was right anyway and say, "Jesus has done nothing wrong, and so I will not allow Him to be punished as if He had." Instead he gave orders that Barabbas was to be let out of prison, and he handed Jesus over to the angry crowd and the soldiers, and they led Him out to crucify Him.

As though that were not enough, they made Him carry the great wooden Cross on which He was to die, until they saw that He would never get to the place where people were crucified if He was not helped.

When they realized this, they called a man who was passing, and made him carry the end of the Cross after our Lord. In the crowd who followed Him there were a great many people who had not joined in asking for Him to be crucified. There were some women there, perhaps some of those He had cured, or whose children He had cured, and they were crying because they were so sorry for Him.

As our Lord went by He turned to them and said, "Do not cry over me, but weep for yourselves and for your children. For such things are to happen here that soon people will be saying that women who have no children are luckier than those who have."

As there were already two men in prison, waiting to be crucified when our Lord was led out to die, the soldiers brought them along, too. When they came to the

place where criminals were put to death, they crucified all three of them; our Lord in the middle and the others, who were thieves, one on each side of Him.

When people were going to be crucified, they were given a drink of wine with drugs in it that made them feel the pain less. But when they gave a cup of it to our Lord, He tasted it but would not drink it.

Then the soldiers pulled His clothes off and laid Him on the Cross. Pilate had written a notice to be nailed to the top of our Lord's Cross, over His head. It was written in the language the Jews spoke, so that they could read it, and in Greek and Latin as well, so that everyone else who could read at all could read it, too. It said, "Jesus of Nazareth, King of the Jews."

When our Lord's enemies saw it, they were very much annoyed, and they went hurrying back to Pilate and said, "You ought not to have written 'The King of the Jews,' but that He *said* He was King of the Jews — please change it!" But Pilate said, "What I have written, I have written." And he would not alter a word.

When our Lord had been nailed to the Cross (for they did nail Him), He kept saying, "Father, forgive them, for they don't know what they are doing."

After the Cross had been set upright in the ground, the soldiers picked up His garments to see what they were worth, for after a man was crucified his clothes belonged to the soldiers who had done it. Each of them took something, but they could not decide which of them was to have His coat, because it was a very good one. I expect our Lady had made it herself, it was all woven in one piece, without any seams. In the end they decided to throw dice for it, and they sat on the ground and did that.

Standing before our Lord's Cross were His Mother and her sister, Mary of Cleophas and Mary Magdalene and St. John, His special friend.

When our Lord looked down and saw them, He said to our Lady, "Behold your son," and then to St. John he said, "Behold your mother." From then on, our Lady and St. John treated each other as mother and son and looked after each other until our Lady died. That was why St. John wrote such a wonderful Gospel. Our Lord loved him best of all the Apostles, and He must have planned from the beginning to leave our Lady in his charge.

Among the people who stood watching our Lord die were many of His enemies. They mocked Him, even on the Cross, and said, "So You could destroy the Temple and build it up again in three days! Why don't You come down from the Cross? So You could save everybody! Why don't You save Yourself?"

And others said, "If You are the King of the Jews, come down from the Cross, and we will believe in You!" and, "He said He trusted in God! Well, if God wants Him, He can save Him now!"

One of the robbers on the other crosses joined in saying, "If You are the Christ, save Yourself and us, too!" But the other one answered, "You ought to fear God, for you are also going to die. Indeed, both of us are, and quite rightly, but this Man has done nothing wrong."

Then he turned his head toward our Lord and said, "Lord, remember me when You come into Your Kingdom." And our Lord answered, "This day you shall be with me in Paradise."

From shortly after our Lord was crucified it began to get dark, and soon it was so dark that everyone began to be afraid, because it was still early afternoon, not nearly time for night to fall.

At three o'clock our Lord cried out in a loud voice, "My God, my God, why hast Thou forsaken me!" Those are the first words of a psalm, and in the Temple in Jerusalem that psalm was just being sung. And, do you know, it is the very one in which King David prophesied the way our Lord was to die? Here are some lines from it:

> All they that saw me
> have laughed me to scorn. . . .
> They have dug my hands and my feet.
> They have numbered all my bones.
> And they have looked and stared upon me.
> They parted my garments amongst them;
> and upon my vesture they cast lots.

That was what the soldiers had just done, wasn't it? The psalm ends like this:

> There shall be declared
> to the Lord a generation to come:
> and the Heavens shall show forth
> His justice to a people that shall be born,
> which the Lord hath made.

And that part of the psalm is about us!

The Roman soldiers standing about did not know anything of this, of course. They thought that our Lord had called Elijah, because in the language our Lord spoke, the word for God and the name Elijah sound rather alike. While they were still looking at Him and wondering that a man who seemed so near to dying could be able to cry out so loud, our Lord said, "I thirst."

One of the soldiers put a sponge into a pitcher of a kind of very thin sour wine, like vinegar, that was standing near, and he set the sponge on the end of a reed and held it to Jesus' lips. The other soldiers said, "Wait, let us see if Elijah will come and take Him down."

When our Lord had drunk the vinegar, He said, "It is finished." Then He cried out in a loud voice, "Father, into Thy hands I commend my spirit."

And He bowed His head down and died.

At the same time, the veil of the Temple, which curtained off the holiest part from the rest, was torn in two, and there was an earthquake, and rocks were broken, and graves were opened and people who had been dead rose again and appeared in Jerusalem. The Roman officer who was in charge of the soldiers by the Cross saw the darkness and felt the earthquake and heard how our Lord cried out before He died, and he said, "Indeed this was the Son of God."

All these things frightened the crowd who had been mocking our Lord and enjoying themselves, and they went home striking their breasts. Our Lord's friends were left alone then, both those standing by the Cross and those who had been standing in the crowd. Among these was Joseph of Arimathea, a man who was one of the council of the ruling Jews, but one who had nothing to do with our Lord's condemnation. In the evening he went to Pilate and asked boldly for our Lord's Body, so that he might give it a proper burial.

Pilate said, "Is He dead already?" And he sent soldiers to make sure.

Other Jews were asking that none of the bodies should be left on the crosses next day, because they said it was not right to have dead bodies hanging on crosses on a holy feast day.

When people had been crucified, if they did not die soon enough, the soldiers used to break their legs, and then they died quickly. So the centurion and some soldiers went out to the three crosses, and they broke the legs of the two thieves, but when they saw that our Lord was already dead, they did not break His legs. But just to make sure, one of the soldiers put his spear into our Lord's side, and water and blood came out.

When Pilate had heard from the soldiers that our Lord was certainly dead, he gave orders that His Body should be given to Joseph of Arimathea, as he had asked. Then Joseph, with some of the others, took our Lord's Body down from the Cross and carried it to a sepulchre, a grave carved out of rock, which was nearby. This was the burying place that Joseph of Arimathea, who was rich, had prepared for his own grave. I do not know why he chose to be buried so close to the place where criminals were killed; perhaps he didn't know either. But we do know that it was in a garden, and it seems to have been in the same garden or on the edge of it that our Lord died. After all, He died to put right everything that once went wrong in a garden, didn't He! For it was in the Garden of Eden that Adam and Eve first set everything going wrong.

When the Jews buried people they used to rub sweet-smelling spices on their bodies and wrap them up in linen cloths instead of putting them in coffins as we do. Nicodemus, who once came to our Lord in the middle of the night because he did not want to be seen, heard what was being done. So he came to the sepulchre bringing a mixture of myrrh and aloes, and with those spices they anointed our Lord's Body, and wrapped it in the linen cloths.

Our Lady was there, and she helped them, and so did Mary Magdalene and Mary of Cleophas. Then they laid our Lord's poor Body down and rolled a great slab of stone against the doorway to close the sepulchre and went home.

Ten

The Resurrection

The next day the Pharisees and the chief priests came to Pilate and said, "Sir, we have remembered that while that seducer was still alive He said, 'After three days I will rise again.' Command that the sepulchre where He is buried shall be guarded until the third day, or perhaps His disciples will come and steal Him away and say He is risen from the dead. That would be worse than ever!" *Seducer* means somebody who leads people astray.

Pilate, who must have been sick of the whole business by now, said, "You have a guard. Go and guard it yourselves. You know perfectly well how to."

So they went to the sepulchre and set a guard of Jewish soldiers over it. Just to make quite sure, they sealed up the stone, so that it could not be moved. You remember how these same people were always making a fuss if our Lord cured a sick man on the Sabbath Day or did almost anything else? Well, this was the Sabbath and a great feast day too, but they thought nothing of doing all this work!

That day our Lord's friends rested and waited for next morning so that they could go back to the sepulchre and finish burying our Lord properly, for they wanted to put more sweet spices on His Body than they had had time for before.

The Jews counted their days from sundown to sundown, so the Sabbath had started on what we would call Friday evening, and they had not had time to finish the burial.

Very early on Sunday morning, as soon as the dawn began to show, Mary Magdalene, Mary of Cleophas, and one or two other women who had followed our Lord set out for the sepulchre.

As they came near to it they said to each other, "Whom can we get to roll back the stone from the door?"

They knew it was too heavy for them, but they did not know that it had been sealed or that a guard of soldiers had been put to stand there. But when they came within sight of the sepulchre, they felt a great earthquake and saw the stone being rolled back by an angel. His face was like lightning, and his clothes like snow, and when the guards saw him they fell down like dead men.

When Mary Magdalene saw all this, she was very frightened and did not understand what was happening. I don't think she saw very well because of crying so much.

She ran back quickly and met Peter and John and said to them, "They have taken the Lord out of the sepulchre, and I don't know where they have laid Him."

But the other women went into the sepulchre after the angel had gone, to make sure our Lord was not there. Of course He was not, but as they were making sure, two more angels who looked like young men in shining clothes came and stood beside them and said, "Do not be afraid. You are looking for Jesus of Nazareth, who was crucified. But He has risen, just as He told you He would. Go and tell His disciples and Peter that He is going to Galilee and there you will see Him."

But they were so startled and frightened, they ran out of the sepulchre, still not understanding whether everything was all right after all, or what had happened. On the way home they did not speak a word to anyone, and I think you can guess how they felt.

When they got near the house where the Apostles were, they began to run, and so came in all breathless, and told what they had seen. But the Apostles were too miserable to understand.

Meantime Peter and John, whom Mary Magdalene had told that our Lord was gone from the sepulchre, were running there as fast as ever they could. John was the younger, and ran the faster, so he reached the sepulchre first and bent down to look through the little door, and he saw that our Lord was not there.

Then Peter came panting up and went into the sepulchre and saw the linen cloths that had been wrapped around our Lord lying just as they had been, but with no one inside, and the piece of linen that had been wrapped around His head was there, wrapped around just as though His head was still in it. John went into the sepulchre, too, and after they were both certain of all they had seen, they came out together and went home.

In the meantime, Mary Magdalene had not gone far away, and now she came back to the sepulchre and stood beside it crying. Still crying, she stooped down and looked through the door. There she saw two angels dressed in white, one sitting at the head and one at the foot of the stone where our Lord's Body had been. One of them said to her, "Woman, why do you weep?"

She answered, "Because they have taken away my Lord, and I do not know where they have laid Him." When she had said this, she turned around and saw our Lord, but what with crying so much, she did not know Him. He said to her, as the angel had, "Woman, why do you weep?"

And she, thinking our Lord was the gardener, said, "Sir, if you have taken Him away from here, tell me where He is, and I will come and take Him away."

Jesus said, "Mary!" And then she recognized Him, and she turned around and clung tightly to His feet and said, "Master!"

Our Lord said, "Do not cling to me so. I am still here! But go now and tell my disciples that I am going into Galilee and that I will meet them there."

Mary Magdalene ran as fast as she could and told the Apostles, but still they could not believe it was anything but a mistake.

In the meantime, the guards who had been set to watch over the sepulchre had come to their senses and gotten away from there as fast as they could. But they did not know what to do next! In the end they agreed that as everything was bound to come out anyway, they had better go to the chief priests themselves and tell them all about it.

The chief priests called a council, and the council decided that anything was better than the truth. So they gave the soldiers a great sum of money and said, "You are to say that you went to sleep while you were on guard and that while you slept the disciples came and stole the body away, and if the governor hears anything about it, we will see that no harm comes to you."

This must have surprised the soldiers — imagine being given money to say they had allowed the very thing to happen which they had been put on guard to prevent! And to say that they were asleep — you know it was then, as it is now, a terrible thing for a soldier to be caught asleep on duty! But I don't know if even they saw how funny it was to be solemnly telling everyone what

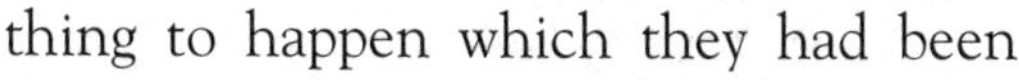

had happened while they were asleep — I wonder if anyone thought of asking them how they knew?

Two of the disciples, who did not yet believe that our Lord had risen, went on a journey that same day. They were going on foot to a town called Emmaus, and expected to get there before evening. As they went along, they talked, as you would expect, of all the things that had been happening in the last three days.

On the way Jesus joined them, but He did not let them know who He was. He said to them, as though He were a stranger, "What are you saying to each other that is so sad?"

One of them answered, "You must have come from a long way off if You do not know what has been happening in Jerusalem!"

Our Lord said, "What has been happening?"

And they answered, "Why, there was a Man called Jesus of Nazareth, who was a prophet and did all kinds of miracles, and we hoped He was the Christ, but the chief priests and Pharisees delivered Him to Pilate to be condemned to death, and on Friday He was crucified. And now, on top of all this, some women went to His sepulchre this morning and said that His Body was not there and that they had seen a vision of angels who said He was alive. And then some of us went to the sepulchre and found His Body was gone, as the women had said, and they could not find Him."

When our Lord had heard all this confused story, He answered, "O foolish and slow of heart to believe what the prophets foretold! Didn't you understand that the Christ had to suffer all these things before He entered into His Glory?"

Then He began to remind them of all the prophecies in the Old Testament about what should happen to Him, beginning with Moses, and going all the way through. When they reached Emmaus, He seemed to intend to go on with His journey alone, but they said to Him, "Stay with us, because it is almost evening; the day is nearly gone."

So He went in with them, and they sat down to supper together. As they sat eating He took bread and blessed it and broke it and gave it to them, and suddenly they recognized Him, and in the same instant He was gone.

Then they said to each other, "Were not our hearts burning within us while He spoke to us on the road and explained the Scriptures?"

Our Lord must have broken the bread just as they remembered seeing Him do it so many times before when He fed thousands with five loaves, and especially at the Last Supper when He gave them the first Holy Communion.

Although it was so late, they got up and went straight back to Jerusalem to tell the Apostles and those who were with them all that had happened.

The Apostles and many of the disciples were gathered together in an upper room, hiding from our Lord's enemies, because they were terrified that it might be their turn to die next. Perhaps the two disciples from Emmaus were still there when Jesus came into the room and was suddenly standing among them, although the doors were shut.

He said, "Peace be to you! It is I. Fear not."

But they were still afraid and did not know if this was their Master or a ghost. When our Lord saw this, He said, "Why are you troubled? See my hands and my feet; it is I myself. You can touch me. A ghost has no flesh and bones, and you can see that I have!"

There were still some there who did not feel sure, so our Lord said, "Have you anything for me to eat?" They offered Him a piece of fish and a honeycomb, and He sat among them and ate. Then they began really to be sure that it was our Lord, and He gave them some of what He was eating to make them surer yet.

When at last there was nothing left in their minds but happiness, no fear at all, He said to them again, "Peace be to you. As my Father has sent me, so I also send you." When He had said this He breathed on them and said, "Receive the Holy Spirit. Whose sins you shall forgive, they are forgiven, and whose sins you do not forgive are not forgiven."

Some people say that He meant the power of forgiving sins to be only for them, but we know that He meant it to be handed on as long as there were sins to forgive, so that we can have our sins forgiven now, just as the first Christians could.

I wonder if you know, or have guessed, why we keep Sunday holy, instead of Saturday? Because our Lord rose from the dead on that day, of course!

The first time our Lord came to the upper room where the disciples were hiding, Thomas was not there. When Thomas came back, the others told him about our Lord's visit, but he would not believe them. He said, "Unless I can see in His hands the mark of the nails, and put my finger into them, and unless I can put my hand into the wound in His side, I will not believe."

A week later, when the doors were shut again, our Lord came a second time and this time Thomas was there. Jesus said, as He had before, "Peace be to you." Then He turned to Thomas and said, "Come here, and see my hands, and put your fingers into the places where the nails were,

and put your hand into the wound where the spear went into my side, and do not be faithless, but believing."

Thomas answered, "My Lord and my God!"

Jesus said, "Because you have seen me, you have believed; blessed are those who have not seen and have believed."

After this Jesus showed Himself again to His disciples beside the Sea of Galilee.

It happened like this: Peter and Thomas, Nathaniel, James and John, and two other disciples were talking together and Peter said, "I am going fishing."

I suppose he was tired of hiding in the upper room and didn't quite know what else to do. The others said to him, "We will go with you."

So they all sailed out into deep water in Peter's boat, and fished all night, but they caught nothing. As they came toward land again in the early morning they saw a man standing on the shore, and He called to them, "Children, have you caught anything?"

They called back, "No."

And He said, "Cast your net on the right side of the boat, and then you will."

They did as He said, and so many fish were caught in it that they could not get it back into the boat. Then John said to Peter, "It is the Lord!"

When Peter heard that, he tied his coat around him, so it wouldn't get in the way, and jumped into the water and swam to land as fast as he possibly could.

The other disciples brought the boat in, still dragging the net full of fish over the side. When they reached the shore they saw a fire burning and a fish broiling on it and bread lying beside it. Then our Lord (because, of course, that is who it was) said, "Bring me some of the fish you have caught." And He put those to cook also and then said, "Come and dine."

The disciples must all have been very hungry, as well as excited. They sat down to eat with Jesus, and none of them dared ask Him if that was who He was.

After they had eaten, our Lord let them know Him plainly, and He said to Peter, "Simon, son of John, do you love me more than these?"

Peter said, "Yes, Lord, You know that I love You."

And our Lord said, "Feed my lambs."

Then He asked him the same thing again, and Peter gave the same answer, and our Lord said the second time, "Feed my lambs."

But when He asked Peter still again if he loved Him, Peter felt miserable that He should still not be sure, and he answered, "Lord, You know all things. You know that I love You!"

And our Lord answered, "Feed my sheep."

Peter had denied our Lord three times — hadn't he? — so our Lord gave him the chance to tell Him three times that he loved Him to make up for it. And in return He gave him charge over all of us, grown-ups and children, bishops and priests, and everyone in the kingdom of God.

After that our Lord gave St. Peter a hint of the way he was to die. He said, "Follow me."

Peter turned around and saw that John was following after him, too, and he said to Jesus, "Lord, what shall this man do?"

Jesus answered, "If I want him to remain until I come, what has that to do with you? Follow me!" Some of the disciples thought this meant that John was not to die until the end of the world. We still don't know what it did mean, although it certainly was not that.

The next to the last time our Lord was seen by the Apostles was in Galilee, too. He had told them to meet Him on a mountain, and there He said, "All power is given me in Heaven and on earth. Go you therefore into the whole world, and preach the Gospel to every creature, baptizing them in the name of the Father and of the Son and of the Holy Spirit, teaching them to observe all things that I have commanded you. And behold, I am with you all days, even to the end of the world."

The very last time of all that He came, they were in Jerusalem. There He made them able to understand the Scriptures and the prophecies about Him, and He told them to wait in the city until they should receive power from Heaven.

Then He walked with them to Bethany on the Mount of Olives where He had raised Lazarus, and where He had been betrayed in the garden. There, on Mount Olivet, He lifted up His hands and blessed them, and as He was still blessing them, He rose up into the sky, and a cloud hid Him.

While they were still looking up after Him, two men in white clothes, who were really angels, stood beside them and said, "You men of Galilee, why do you stand looking up to Heaven? This Jesus who is taken up from you into Heaven shall come in the same way as you have seen Him go."

Then they went back to Jerusalem and prayed and waited, as our Lord had told them to.

Eleven

The Kingdom Is the Church

Well, our Lord had done all that He came to do and had gone back to Heaven. He had died for us and had left His Kingdom in the world — a very small Kingdom, all ready to grow — but for a little while it didn't grow. The Apostles and the disciples and our Lady all waited in the same upper room where they had gone to hide after our Lord was betrayed.

What were the Apostles waiting for? They knew what to say, and what to do, but there was still something that they needed.

Our Lord had told them that the Holy Spirit would come and strengthen them. So they prayed and waited, for until He came they did not feel at all like going out to preach and getting themselves hurt and killed!

Ten days later, that is, fifty days after Easter Sunday, as they were all praying, there came a sound like a rushing wind, and it filled the house where they were sitting.

At the same time there appeared to them parted tongues, like tongues of fire, which rested on every one of them. And they suddenly found that they had courage for anything and that they could speak all kinds of languages that they had not learned.

Immediately they went running straight out of the house into the street and they preached about our Lord to whoever would listen. At that time, there were people in Jerusalem from every nation that the Jews had ever heard of, and the extraordinary thing is that every one of them heard them preaching in his own language!

Now that was really the birthday of the Kingdom, and it is called *Pentecost*, which means "fiftieth," because it happened on the fiftieth day from Easter Day.

Ever since then, the work of teaching the whole world has been going on. Of course, it takes a long time, especially as parts of the world have a way of coming unconverted as soon as you turn your back.

Altogether there is plenty more work to do before the whole world has heard about our Lord. That is why you must learn all you can about your King and His Kingdom so that you can do your part.

It would be awful if one day our Lord said to us, "What did you do about spreading my Kingdom?" and we had to say, "Nothing at all!"

Wouldn't it?

Biographical Note

Marigold Hunt was a speaker for the Catholic Evidence Guild and served for many years as advertising manager of Sheed and Ward publishing company. In addition to this book, she wrote *St. Patrick's Summer*, *A Book of Angels*, and *The First Christians: The Acts of the Apostles for Children*.

Marigold Hunt spent her final years in Somerset, Massachusetts, with her friends Patricia and Owen McGowan. She died on December 15, 1994, and is buried in St. Patrick's Cemetery in Somerset.

Sophia Institute

Sophia Institute is a nonprofit institution that seeks to nurture the spiritual, moral, and cultural life of souls and to spread the Gospel of Christ in conformity with the authentic teachings of the Roman Catholic Church.

Sophia Institute Press fulfills this mission by offering translations, reprints, and new publications that afford readers a rich source of the enduring wisdom of mankind.

Sophia Institute also operates two popular online Catholic resources: CrisisMagazine.com and CatholicExchange.com.

Crisis Magazine provides insightful cultural analysis that arms readers with the arguments necessary for navigating the ideological and theological minefields of the day. *Catholic Exchange* provides world news from a Catholic perspective as well as daily devotionals and articles that will help you to grow in holiness and live a life consistent with the teachings of the Church.

In 2013, Sophia Institute launched Sophia Institute for Teachers to renew and rebuild Catholic culture through service to Catholic education. With the goal of nurturing the spiritual, moral, and cultural life of souls, and an abiding respect for the role and work of teachers, we strive to provide materials and programs that are at once enlightening to the mind and ennobling to the heart; faithful and complete, as well as useful and practical.

Sophia Institute gratefully recognizes the Solidarity Association for preserving and encouraging the growth of our apostolate over the course of many years. Without their generous and timely support, this book would not be in your hands.

www.SophiaInstitute.com
www.CatholicExchange.com
www.CrisisMagazine.com
www.SophiaInstituteforTeachers.org